THREE MANY COOKS

*One Mom,
Two Daughters:
Their Shared
Stories
of Food, Faith
& Family*

Three Many Cooks

**PAM ANDERSON, MAGGY KEET
& SHARON DAMELIO**

BALLANTINE BOOKS

NEW YORK

Published in the United States by Ballantine Books,
an imprint of Random House, a division of Random House LLC,
a Penguin Random House Company, New York.

BALLANTINE and the HOUSE colophon are
registered trademarks of Random House LLC.

LIBRARY OF CONGRESS CATALOGING-IN-PUBLICATION DATA
Anderson, Pam.
Three many cooks : one mom, two daughters : their shared stories of
food, faith & family / Pam Anderson, Maggy Keet, Sharon Damelio.
pages cm
ISBN 978-0-8041-7895-2 (hardback)—
ISBN 978-0-8041-7897-6 (eBook)
1. Anderson, Pam, 1957–   2. Keet, Maggy.   3. Damelio, Sharon.
4. Cooks—United States—Biography.   5. Cooking—Anecdotes.
I. Keet, Maggie.   II. Damelio, Sharon.   III. Title.
TX649.A1A53 2015
641.5092'2—dc23   2014038602

Printed in the United States of America on acid-free paper

www.ballantinebooks.com

2 4 6 8 9 7 5 3 1

FIRST EDITION

Book design by Barbara M. Bachman

Contents

•

Recipes

Introduction

SOME PEOPLE PLAN WHAT THEY ARE GOING TO DO WHEN they get together; our family plans what we are going to eat. Pam and her husband, David, both grew up in households where food was revered and big meals were the main event. Then they had Maggy and Sharon, who happily clung to their mother's apron strings, eating and learning in her busy kitchen. Maggy married Andy, Sharon married Anthony, and the love affair with cooking and eating became a family passion.

Last Memorial Day, the six of us were going to be together for the first time in six months. We had three days and four nights together just waiting to be filled with great food, sublime wines, and killer cocktails. Since half the pleasure is in the yearning, we began plotting and relishing each breakfast, lunch, cocktail hour, and dinner.

Pam, who was hosting the whole group, started the email chain weeks in advance, inviting ideas and cravings. After an initial flurry of food fantasies, Sharon cut and pasted everything into a Word document, which started whizzing back and forth with edits. Bargaining commenced.

"Can we switch fried chicken to Saturday dinner? No one wants to eat cold chicken at a picnic."

"Wild mushroom chowder feels heavy for our first night, so what about Italian Wedding Soup?"

"Gin and tonics are boring and I've got loads of fresh mint. Let's make juleps for Friday's cocktail hour."

Fifty-three. That's how many emails it takes three cooks—a mother and her two adult daughters—to figure out what they are going to make and savor over one long weekend.

Perhaps we are slightly obsessive about eating and drinking. Maybe we need a shrink to tell us that letting food shape every aspect of our lives together and apart isn't "normal." But it's probably too late for therapy. We love food, period. Pam is a veteran cookbook author, and all three of us run the food blog Three Many Cooks. But it's more than that.

We cook (and eat!) because it brings us incredible joy. Because sitting down to a meal we've made—whether it's Southern fried chicken, quinoa salad, or a dry martini and a pile of cheese and crackers—gives us plain and simple pleasure. We cook because nothing compares to the scent of onions and garlic sautéing in olive oil, and because we secretly love the scars on our hands (and the accompanying stories) that prove we're culinary warriors. We cook because the best conversations always happen when we've got a piece of counter space, a sharp knife, a stiff drink, and a job to do. And because somehow the ability to nourish ourselves and others makes us feel humble and powerful at the same time.

We cook because we come from a long line of men and women who showed us the value of good food shared, people who—despite our flaws and differences—could always find common ground cutting into a homemade cake and having a cup of coffee. When we're in the kitchen making the dishes they taught us from memory, we can feel that cloud of witnesses hovering over us—reminding us to leave the butter in the freezer just a little bit longer before making that piecrust, giving us the side-eye when we try to make it too fancy, smiling as we wash our ziplock bags to reuse them (again), and urging us to "just get in there and do it, already" when we don't feel like cooking much of anything.

We cook, finally, because we feel a deep need to do it. We are women with an innate desire to feed people, and of that we are not ashamed.

This book is a collection of stories about our incredible, messy, hilarious, powerful, screwed-up, delicious, and life-changing love affair with food, with one another, and with the people we have come to cherish. It's full of stories that explore our past and present, from the sweltering farms of central Alabama and the white dunes of the Florida Panhandle to the quiet woods of Bucks County, Pennsylvania; from the humming streets of Chicago and New York City to the sunny strangeness of southern France and Malawi. Over a handful of decades and in dozens of kitchens, we have made the moments and the meals that have shaped us. Along with our stories, we offer the recipes that really mean something to us—the ones we can't live without, the ones we can't wait to share, the ones that are so simple it seems silly, and the ones that we still can't believe we have mastered.

Glorious food is sometimes the most important aspect of an experience. More often it's little more than the catalyst for the really good stuff—great laughs, long talks, strong relationships. As diligently as we planned that Memorial Day weekend, life intervened. When Sharon and Anthony's flight got delayed first by minutes, then by hours, and then finally diverted to another airport, we resigned ourselves to the fact that the cozy and relaxing evening of homemade soup, bread, fresh fruit, and plentiful wine was a fantasy.

When everyone finally arrived bleary-eyed at the house it was close to midnight. We could have simply opted to collapse into our beds and save the celebrating for more civil hours, but we didn't. We all knew our parts in this ongoing story, and we got to work. Pam and Maggy went to the kitchen to assemble a gorgeous board of cheeses, olives, and meats. David set to work washing the prep dishes, while Andy cued up some good music. Sharon started unpacking the goodies she'd brought from down South, and Anthony headed straight for the bar to start mixing up cocktails for the group.

By the time we all gathered around the coffee table by the fireplace, half of us sitting on couches and the other half on the floor, it was nearly 1:00 A.M. Fatigue be damned, we all raised a glass to making plans and breaking them and to all the meals, great and small, that bring us together.

In our experience, a meaningful life doesn't just happen. You have to build it with the blocks you have. Blocks from the past and present, ones that represent moments of both light and shadow. Though we've got plenty of materials for building, most of our blocks are made of simple stuff: food, family, and faith.

As writers, we've discovered that we only find real meaning as we write it—turning ideas over in our heads, plucking the perfect word from the air, reliving the moment in print. As cooks, our lives just don't seem real or right unless we're making food that nourishes us and the ones we love. Our greatest moments wouldn't be the same without the meals that made them happen, or the people who taught us how to cook. Loving food and words, almost in equal measure, we have come to understand who we are and what we're doing on this blue-green marble by cooking our way to good food and strong family, and then writing about it. This collection of stories and recipes is our attempt to put the pieces together. We invite you to join us and, ultimately, to do the same.

THREE MANY COOKS

/.

History of a Cook

pam

AS A VETERAN FOOD WRITER AND RECIPE DEVELOPER, I am often asked how I learned to cook. My grandmother, mother, and aunt—all Southern women from the last century—were accomplished cooks and taught me to follow suit. But it was my father who taught me how to eat, how to relish a meal, how to savor friends and family, have one more helping, steal one last morsel. Oddly—or perhaps inevitably—it was my father, a recovering alcoholic since before I was born, who taught me how to drink. Not by ever offering me a glass of Cabernet with my steak, but by helping me to embrace a world of big, bold flavors around a rollicking table, so that my love of food and wine was assured.

All of that came later, however. As a child, I learned to cook in three distinctly Southern kitchens—one on the Florida Panhandle and two in southern Alabama—at the elbow of those women, beginning with my mother. Mom didn't love the kitchen, but she was a good Southern woman, which

meant she cooked. Every day. Never a breakfast person herself, she ritually served up the Southern classic plate of
bacon, eggs, grits, and toast for Dad and me every morning.
For herself, she'd fold a piece of dry toast over a strip of
bacon or sausage for what she called a "bend-over sandwich." Her favorite breakfast was leftover garlic toast from
one of Dad's grilled dinners the night before. I was never
sure whether she loved the garlic toast or just felt good about
getting rid of something no one else wanted to eat.

Following in the farming tradition, where they serve
their big meal midday, Mom started preparing lunch right
after breakfast. "Dinner," we called it. She didn't quite have
a set menu for each day of the week, but she definitely had
her standard meat-and-three repertoire. Lots of chicken—
with dressing, with dumplings. Plenty of fried—fish, pork
chops, and more chicken. She slow cooked pot roast at least
once a week.

Our vegetables, always wonderfully long-simmered and
pork-flavored, rarely changed. On summer trips back from
Mama Skipper and Grandaddy's farm in Alabama, I'd sit in
the front seat between Mom and Dad to make room for the
sheet-covered backseat mounded with fresh field peas, corn,
butterbeans, and okra, which we shelled and shucked and
cut until we regretted our greediness. What we didn't enjoy
right away got put up in the Buick-size chest freezer, which
ate up half our patio. Throughout winter Mom would supplement our seasonal collards, mustard greens, rutabagas,
and turnips with a package of summer's treasures from the
deep freeze.

There was a pan of hot corn bread at nearly every meal, and at least three times a week Mom made meringue pie, banana pudding, or one of her famous chocolate, coconut, or caramel cakes. When the homemade dessert ran out, there was always a carton of ice cream, which she and I would finish off together as a reward for defrosting the freezer.

Dad, who was the building inspector for our little town and never more than a ten-minute drive away, came home at noon. Before I started school, and then during summer breaks, the three of us sat down together for "dinner," the sumptuous noon feast. Frequently Mom and Dad would entertain missionaries or an evangelist preaching at our church, and Dad would pick me up from school so I could share the meal with these honored guests. In our little-town version of Mayberry, we were fascinated by missionaries on furlough from Pakistan who could say, "Good morning" and quote John 3:16 in Urdu. This was about the only time my very practical mother ever bothered to set the table with a starched tablecloth and napkins, along with her china, crystal, and silver.

After the morning chore of getting the big meal on the table, Mom could relax a little. She might need to slice up some tomatoes or make another gallon of iced tea, but supper was simply warmed-up leftovers from the big meal.

People often define themselves as cooks or bakers. For Mom, there was no such distinction—it was all the same to her—but her cautious, methodical personality made her a fine baker. She was most content in the kitchen standing next to her whirring mixer, cake batter poised to pour into waxed paper–lined cake pans. Mom's oldest sister, Juliaette, recognized her talent and often tasked her with baking cakes for our big family gatherings.

Mom was the youngest of ten siblings—five sisters, five brothers—who all lived in Alabama. For the holidays our little family of three, along with everyone else, gathered at the home of the family-appointed matriarch, Aunt Juliaette. She was queen of her bustling kitchen, and the younger sisters took orders, moving from duty in her kitchen to breaks around her table, a dance that started early morning and didn't stop until we went to bed. We all squeezed in at the table for meals, but in between there was always a gathered cluster whispering family secrets or telling well-worn stories, nibbling on sweets and smoking cigarettes, always with a cup of coffee or glass of iced tea in hand.

Aunt Juliaette was both a forceful cook and a solid baker. Accordingly, she was bossy, opinionated, and a little prickly. She was the first to see the budding cook in me, and at a young age I made it into her culinary inner circle. For my first cooking lesson she handed me an onion and asked me to peel and chop it. As I tried carefully to slip off the paper-thin layer, I half expected her to bark at me for taking so long. Instead, she tenderly suggested it'd go much faster if I just pulled off the first layer of flesh along with the tissue-y skin. She was gently amused watching the tears stream down my cheeks as I chopped. She died before I got my first cooking job, but I think she would have been proud.

We shared our holiday time with Mama Skipper and Grandaddy, Dad's parents who lived about thirty miles south of Montgomery in La Pine. Whereas Montgomery was Alabama's second largest city, La Pine was a town of a hundred dirt farmers. My paternal grandparents lived in a shack that had been added on to and gussied up into a "house," but it was still primitive. The electrical system was a spiderweb of extension cords over ceilings and uninsulated walls. A real bathroom had been added on, but my grandfather considered it a womanly concession to modernity and refused to use it. He shaved from a bowl on the back porch and did his business in the outhouse.

Visits to my grandmother's simple kitchen were always memorable. Annie Skipper was a gifted country cook. Like Aunt Juliaette, Mama Skipper must have intuited a fellow cook because she patiently taught me how to pan-fry chicken in a cast-iron skillet that she covered with a borrowed glass lid from another pan, and how to make biscuits from the ready bowl of flour stored underneath the open counter. I watched as she mixed in lard and buttermilk by sight and feel. As she dropped the free-form balls of dough into the pan, it was my job to knuckle them into plump discs.

As a child I never understood why Mom called her mother-in-law "Mrs. Skipper." Only later did I find out she was not Mama Skipper's first choice for her son. Nevertheless, Mama Skipper ritually welcomed us with a batch of her fried apple or peach hand pies, which she knew my mother adored. On the few occasions she made them after we arrived, she let me fork-seal them before she slid them into the skillet.

My mother, my aunt, my grandmother, these were the women who taught me how to cook. For the first twenty years of my life in the food world, I was busy learning how to create not just the "simple" food of my Southern heritage, but—as I imagined—more sophisticated cuisines. My new teachers were masters like Child, Beard, and Claiborne. Instead of fried chicken and coconut cakes it was daubes and pâté brisée, but it was the same as standing beside Mom or Juliaette or Mama Skipper. I thought it was important to master recipes and techniques. I called my first book *The Perfect Recipe*, and three of my next six books all featured "perfect" somewhere in the title.

A little later in life I started caring less about how "good" my food was and more about how people enjoyed themselves at my table. In other words, I became less like my mother and more like my father, less of a cook and more of an eater. I knew I needed someone to teach me how to cook. Finding that teacher was easy. But when I wanted to learn how to eat, I was surprised to look inside and see within me a man in a sleeveless T-shirt, work pants, and suspenders, standing over a smoking grill.

Until his retirement Dad didn't spend much time in the kitchen, but he ruled at all forms of outdoor cooking. During the week he may have been a building inspector, but on the weekend, the chef and maître d' in him came alive. He was the force behind all of our family gatherings and neighborhood parties. He looked for reasons to light a mound of charcoal and grill a few steaks. He looked forward to his days on the boat, but what he really loved was frying up his catch.

On a hot July day he'd buy the biggest basket of peaches he could find. Sometimes he and Mom would make a big canister of homemade peach ice cream. Other times he'd sit on the patio with his pocketknife, start peeling away the fuzzy skin, and pass them around to eat. Either way the neighbors would descend like flies to honey.

Dad was most famous for his lemon chicken, but regardless of what he threw on the grill, Mom's accompaniments, which she splendidly mastered and dutifully made, never changed. More vegetable than lettuce, her iceberg salads were equal part tomato and carrot, green pepper and radish. In the later years she switched to bottled dressing, but at an early age I learned from her how to dress a salad with oil and vinegar.

Dad would time lighting the grill to Mom's sliding her foil-wrapped potatoes and onions into the hot oven. An hour later the steamy packets would emerge, the sweet onions hidden between thick potato slices now soft as marrow. As Dad was pulling the chicken off the fire, she'd hand him a basket of buttery white loaf bread laced with garlic salt to toast on the grill.

Mom was a good sous chef; she made sure the chef had his mis. Even now I can hear him yell out from the backyard, "Della Ruth! Where's my basting brush?" Or "I need paper towels!" Mom would wearily come out and point to it all. He'd always have a good reason why he hadn't seen it.

Dad was a confident griller, but he was a little insecure about his lemon chicken. Sometimes the lemon flavor was pleasantly faint, while other times it tasted as if the sauce had penetrated down to the bone. Dad always aimed for the latter, but he was never quite sure how to control the outcome.

Needing a little affirmation before he took the chicken off the grill, he'd break off a wing for me to taste test. Not wanting to disappoint, I always assured him it was perfect, complete with sound effects, lip licking, and eye rolling, but he could read the truth in my eyes. (Never trust a hungry ten-year-old.) The grill lid would fly open and he'd begin basting again, hoping his fire would stay alive long enough to get a few more drops of lemon sauce onto the chicken.

Dipping the chicken into the leftover basting sauce was my favorite way to ensure puckery flavor (who worried about salmonella back then?) but to Dad it meant failure. When he saw me sneak the leftover sauce to the table and slip a piece of my breast meat into the bowl, he'd blame himself.

He tried a number of experiments over the years, but it wasn't until one night soon after I'd left home that he called as giddy as a scratch-ticket winner. "I've finally discovered the secret to perfect lemon chicken," he exclaimed. He was frying fish, he said, and toward the end his oil cooled off. His last batch of fish was greasy, and he finally made the connection. What had been bad for his fish might be good for his chicken. Next time, instead of basting the parts from start to finish as usual, he simply threw the chicken parts on the grill and cooked them until they were virtually done. Then he took the fire down really low and started brushing them with the sauce. Eureka.

For years we continued to enjoy Dad's lemon chicken. Even though he had cracked the code, he still needed our reassurance that the chicken was just right. I can still recite our little culinary liturgy.

CHEF: This chicken doesn't taste lemony at all.

RESPONSE: What are you talking about? The lemon flavor has penetrated the chicken right down to the bone.

CHEF: You think so? Mine doesn't taste very lemony.

RESPONSE: Are you kidding? You must've gotten lucky again—this is the best lemon chicken ever.

He'd shrug it off, but he was pleased. We had told him all he needed to hear.

Dad grilled his last lemon chicken on Memorial Day 2012. Earlier that month, with cancer bedeviling my mother and my father losing his memory, I had moved them into a retirement facility. After the mess and trauma of moving they were ready for something enjoyable, so our family— Sharon and Anthony, Maggy and Andy, and David—joined me in Florida for the holiday weekend to celebrate Granny and Papa's new digs and to help say good-bye to their home of thirty-five years.

By the time David and the kids came down, I had already managed the major furniture transport to Mathison Retirement Center. Still, everyone wanted to gather one last time at the home Mom and Dad had built on Deer Point Lake. The place looked like it had been tossed. Everything worth taking had been moved to the new apartment. All that was left at the old place were some random furniture, knick-knacks that hadn't made the cut, and stuff we hoped would attract bargain hunters at our upcoming tag sale. Depression-era babies, Mom and Dad waste little and part with even less, so it had been a hard day of negotiating what more they could take to Mathison and what had to be left for the sale or (though it was never actually said) tossed in the dumpster. By the end, Dad had had it. He was confused, frustrated, and angry.

Our meal plan for the day was to cook up as many freezer treasures as possible. Scrounging for dinner, we found a big pack of chicken legs and thighs and a ziplock bag filled with fresh squeezed lemon juice. Bingo. We'd get Dad to make his famous lemon chicken. One last time.

David pulled the grill out of the toolshed and set it up in the shade. He got a chair so Dad could sit. Then he and the kids headed off to the store for a few last-minute ingredients. Just like the old days, it was just Mom, Dad, and me left to make the meal.

But it wasn't like old times. With all the day's activity Mom's chemo-infused body was worn out. She lay on one of the remaining couches like a bird in shock: body perfectly still, eyes darting around the room as if spying for predators. As I performed Mom's role as sous chef, I looked out in the backyard to check on Dad. His chicken was on fire, and he was just standing there. He didn't know what to do. I raced out and doused the fire. The chicken had almost charred, but with a little babying, it was salvageable. The shopping crew returned, and the rest of dinner prep went smoothly.

That night we finally sat down to dinner, exhausted. We unwrapped our foiled potatoes and onions, tender and caramel-bottomed. We served up oil-and-vinegar tossed salad, just the way Mom used to do it. We made toast her way, too, garlicky and potent. As far as the chicken went, I was prepared to sing my part in the old duet. But on a day when my father actually had good reason to declare his chicken subpar, he took one bite and said, "This turned out a lot better than I thought it would." In my heart I was pleased he was content, but my head was telling me my father's poor mind was going fast.

During my monthly visits the following year I witnessed Dad's steady mental decline. To compound his troubles, the unrelenting pressure that had made him near-blind in one eye was now rising dangerously in his other one.

Late April the lights went out, which marked the beginning of Dad's short end. He went blind. He stopped eating, a man who had had a lifelong affair with food. When the health-care workers called with this news, I quickly made my way down to Florida. Seeing the insipid institutional food on his plate I couldn't blame a Southern man on hunger strike. I got up early the next morning, made cheese grits, and carried them to the nursing center where he'd been moved. I spoon-fed him, and he ate my grits like a hungry baby. As an only child who lives a thousand miles to the north, I had the momentary delusion that I could quit my life and career and live down there so that I could cook the kind of food my father loved and spoon-feed him every day until he was back to his old self. When reality returned, I cried a little, got on a plane, and flew home.

Two days later, Dad's attendant called to say he was not breathing right, and they were taking him to the hospital. I considered heading for the airport, but held off. The next day, at four in the morning, a nurse called. My father had pneumonia. She recommended hospice. I caught a morning flight.

Sharon picked me up in Atlanta, and we drove the rest of the way to Panama City, Florida. Late afternoon we arrived at the hospital. Unconscious, Dad's body convulsed erratically as he labored to breathe. We sang, we prayed, we read Psalms, we kissed, we hugged. Hospice took over, and for the next three days Sharon and I midwifed Dad as he labored to his death. The night we thought his heart would finally give out, we set up a cot next to his bed for Mom. With his bride lying beside him, Dad died shortly after midnight.

There was no family home anymore, so we all gathered at a rented condominium on Panama City Beach. There was a lot to figure out in a short time, and it felt odd but right when the girls and their spouses quietly excused themselves and started taking charge. Sharon and Anthony and Maggy and Andy traded off handling meals and loving on my mom, while David worked quietly on Dad's eulogy.

The funeral was on Mother's Day. Dad had been in decline so long I needed to be reminded of the vibrant man David eulogized. Flynn Collins Skipper, he said, was king of the grill, lord of the fish fry, master of the ice cream freezer. A host who wanted everyone to savor great food and most of all, as he always said, "Have a big time!"

After the service we proceeded in cars to Oakland Cemetery. As the funeral director pushed a button and my father's coffin sank slowly into its grave, I wondered what could I pull out of this man before they shoveled dirt in his face. What of his life might live on in me? I knew what it was. Once he swore off booze the only thing he really had to give was his passion for food and his natural gift of big hospitality.

Unlike Mom's style, which was dutiful and serviceable, Dad's way was big and bold, generous and messy. He was the one who argued for throwing that extra steak on the grill, whose night was made when everyone ate until they groaned. His way of cooking and eating had been passed on to me, the way he would hold out a morsel of lemon chicken when I couldn't wait until the whole thing was off the grill and on the table—he would tear off a blackened bit of wing, hold it out like the bread of heaven, and I would eat it from his hand.

After the burial David and I carefully squired my mom back to the rented condo and the makeshift family reception while the kids went shopping. In short order Sharon and Anthony, Maggy and Andy all walked into the place saddled with oversized bags of more meats and cheeses than we could possibly eat and two bags of clinking bottles—wine, as the Psalm has it, to "make our hearts glad."

Together, Maggy and Sharon presented me with a gin and tonic in some glass from the rented kitchen cupboard, the tallest I have ever seen, smelling of lime and "perfumed" with a capful of Bombay Sapphire splashed on top. I realized Dad had passed on his big living to them, too. They knew it, and they smiled.

Grilled Lemon Chicken

SERVES 8

Grilled Lemon Chicken was my dad's signature dish. Over the years he made it hundreds of times and was frustrated that sometimes the lemon flavor would penetrate the chicken and other times it wouldn't. After much testing, he finally figured out that for a bright, fresh lemon flavor, submerge the chicken in a lemon/garlic/oil mixture at the end of cooking—genius. The 1½ hour brining time is nice, but not essential; skip it if you're in a hurry (or using a kosher chicken). If you like, add 1 tablespoon of minced fresh thyme or rosemary to the lemon marinade.

Salt and ground black pepper

2 (3 ½ to 4-pound) whole chickens, each cut into 10 pieces (4 breast pieces, 2 drumsticks, 2 thighs, 2 wings)

6 garlic cloves, minced to a paste

¼ cup olive oil

1 cup lemon juice

Dissolve ½ cup salt in 2 quarts cold water in a large container. Submerge chicken in brine, cover, and refrigerate for 1½ hours. Remove chicken from brine, rinse, and pat dry. Sprinkle with pepper.

Mix garlic, oil, and lemon juice in a bowl; set aside.

Heat a gas grill, igniting all burners on high for at least 10 minutes or build a hot charcoal fire. Use a wire brush to clean the grill rack, then wipe a vegetable oil–soaked rag over grill rack. Close lid to return grill to high temperature. Have water close by to extinguish any flare-ups.

Place chicken parts, skin side down, on hot grill rack. Cover and grill until well browned on both sides, turning once about half-way through and extinguishing flames as necessary, 15 to 20 minutes. Turn burners to medium-low, and working a few pieces at a time, place chicken in lemon mixture and turn to thoroughly coat. Return to grill. Continue to cook until a meat thermometer confirms that parts are done (160°F for breasts and 170°F for legs and thighs), brushing with excess lemon mixture as the chicken continues to cook, 5 to 10 minutes longer. Transfer to a platter and serve.

Three Many Cooks
in the Kitchen

maggy

OFTEN WONDER HOW MY MOM FELT WHEN SHE REALIZED HER firstborn daughter was simply not interested in cooking. I was happy to top pizzas, decorate cookies, and lick frosting bowls until streaky clean, but I vividly remember the first time she tried to impart some real cooking knowledge. I'm sorry to say that what she'd probably imagined as a triumphant moment of motherhood was a total bust.

When she called me into the kitchen that Saturday afternoon, I was already rolling my eyes as I dragged myself through the swinging door. I looked at her impatiently, waiting for her to assign a chore. Instead she directed my gaze to the counter. I must have been eight because my blond bangs only just came above the counter.

There on a rimmed baking sheet lay a raw, butterflied chicken. Mom had made long, shallow slits in the chicken's breasts, thighs, and legs and was in the process of rubbing some kind of herbed paste she'd made between the meat and the skin. "Maggy, I just wanted to show you how to season a chicken like this. You see how I've made these slits?" she said as she pushed her hand under the skin, breaking away the silky, viscous layer attaching skin to meat. This looked more like an autopsy than dinner prep. "See how that creates a pocket in there? This paste is going to roast into the meat and make the chicken really flavorful."

I nodded and smiled, quickly considering which response would get me out of the kitchen faster. I settled on a "Yup, looks good!" More clearly than the memory of watching her slit and stuff that chicken, I remember exactly how I felt: apathetic. She sensed it, too.

And so it continued throughout my childhood, Mom trying to gently nudge me toward the kitchen while I politely veered away. I was a great eater. Raw oysters, bouillabaisse, pâté? No problem! I had an appreciation for what came from the kitchen and the eating and togetherness that ensued, but beyond cake decorating and pancake flipping, I was simply not interested in how real food was made. Sharon, however, was immediately at home at the stove. She was always at Mom's heels, helping and learning. Throughout those elementary and high school years, people often assumed, "With your mom being such a good cook, you must love cooking, too!" It happened so often I had a canned response ready: "Not really. She's always made such good food I've never needed to!" Not unlike the cobbler's children who found themselves without shoes, I was the cook's kid with no idea (or interest in) how to cook. It wasn't for Mom's lack of trying, but I had to find my own way into the kitchen. And it wasn't through the front door.

The college years and a nine-month stint at home before getting married were a blur of cafeteria meals and hastily assembled sandwiches, but when Andy and I returned to England after our honeymoon to set up our home, my culinary deficiency became glaring. After growing up in Mom's kitchen, I knew what good food should taste like; I just didn't know how to make it.

At the time I could make a few basics—chicken fajitas, spaghetti Bolognese, sausages and mash and, with the help of jars and packets, lasagna and chili. You get those things on rotation, and it's not long before you get bored and realize there's a big difference between food that fills the hole and food that nourishes the soul. There is, of course, a yawning chasm between chicken noodle soup from a can, flat and tinny, and homemade chicken soup made with fresh onions, carrots, and celery, slow-simmered stock, and meat just pulled from the bone. Oddly, it wasn't until I wandered 3,500 miles away from her that I began to see the first hint of "Mom, the Cook" in me. Despite all her nudging, it was my urge to nourish my new husband and myself that ultimately led me to the kitchen—this time to make real food. I set out to cook all the things I had eaten for years at home, the stuff of great meals whose every taste I knew by heart.

Time was short, and the learning curve was steep. I was in graduate school full-time getting my master's degree in international development, commuting to and from London several days a week, while also fund-raising and planning for the maternity clinic I had promised to build in Malawi. To make ends meet, I was working part-time behind the bar at our local pub. Despite my frenetic schedule, I made dinner a priority, and I was getting decent food on the table. My culinary education was under way.

Often, I messed up. Like the time I got beautiful thick-cut pork chops from the butcher for a dinner party. I planned to sear the chops and serve them with a pan sauce, mashed potatoes, and vegetables. I knew that getting a good sear required a really hot skillet, but my pan was so hot that I burned the chops trying to get them cooked through. Sure, I was an amateur cook, but I knew that pork chops—unlike beefsteaks—weren't meant to be bright pink on the inside. By the time the meat had reached a safe internal temperature, the whole meal had devolved into an overcooked mess. The skillet was coated with burned bits, not the caramelized goodness Mom always transfigured into rich, golden pan sauces. Our guests smiled and nodded as they worked out their jaws, chewing each overcooked bite about fifty times before swallowing. I looked on, mortified, trying to remember how to do the Heimlich maneuver should it come to that.

Then there was the time I attempted to make slow cooker chili that came out with a consistency akin to cat food. I couldn't understand what I had done wrong—throw it all in, turn it on, and leave it alone for five hours, just like the recipe said. How do you mess that up? Money was tight, and we lived in a small, rural town with few restaurants. When I botched dinner we couldn't go out, so we kept emergency cans of Heinz tomato soup on hand that we ate with slices of buttered bread. I continued to make attempts in the kitchen, and with each failure came an important lesson and often a call to Mom to talk about what had gone wrong. I could sense in her trans-Atlantic voice that she was quietly thrilled that I was learning. Instead of getting me sweaters and DVDs for Christmas, she gave me a large Le Creuset Dutch oven, a Henckels knife set, and a roasting pan.

As my interest grew, I checked out cookbooks from our local library and, for the first time in my life, started reading and cooking from the books my own mother had written. But I knew from Mom that while recipes were important, a cook shouldn't be dependent on them. I spent the next few years internalizing formulas and basic recipes, finally getting comfortable enough to riff. I may have been an apathetic student, but all Mom's efforts weren't for naught—that latent knowledge bubbled up at the first sign of nurturing. Amid a few memorable failures, cooking began to come naturally and quickly.

I delved deeper into my family's food traditions. Instead of arriving on time for dinner at Andy's grandparents' house, we'd show up early so I could watch his grandmother cook, learning how to make her Marmite gravy and the method for her crispy duck fat–roasted potatoes. When I visited my own grandparents, I started jotting down their recipes for chicken tetrazzini and sugar cookies on scraps of curled-up paper.

What I learned was twofold. I was learning to cook, but I was also learning firsthand the power of food that my mom had been creating my whole life. I loved watching our friends devour appetizers and wine around our faux fireplace, nestled into our overstuffed couches with music in the background and surrounded by the hum of conversation. In this environment, our friends started telling stories that never came out in loud, crowded restaurants and bars. As we retrieved coats and embraced by the front door at the end of the night, I loved knowing that we had reached a new level of intimacy and friendship. When Andy and I moved to Africa, I marveled at the same sense of community that was shared around an open fire, on a bamboo mat, or by the community well. More and more, food revealed itself to be so much more than what we eat.

You can be the recipient of the goodness that comes from food, but you have to create it yourself to really "get" on a deeper level the way that home-cooked meals and relationship-building are inextricably linked.

By the time Andy and I moved to New York City, I was a passionate home cook and a perennial baker. Sharon, Mom, and I had not been together on a regular basis since I'd left for college in 2001. But now, Sharon was in Connecticut at Yale Divinity School and Mom was just forty-five minutes away in Darien. Gatherings were frequent and always kitchencentric. In this new family kitchen of Three Many Cooks, a hierarchy emerged—of which I was clearly the third. Mom and Sharon were a twosome and I was the odd one out.

I had learned a lot about food in the five years since Andy and I were married, but Sharon, who had always been inspired in the kitchen, now had two years at *Fine Cooking* magazine under her belt. Mom jokes that she got her culinary PhD during her years at *Cook's* magazine, and Sharon

followed suit, passion and intuition fortified with a magazine education. The more we cooked together, the more our
styles and roles emerged. There weren't too many cooks in
the kitchen—two cooks worked just fine. But I was the third
cook, and my role was definitely a supporting one.

I could hardly complain. If Sharon got Mom's passion for
cooking in her DNA, then I got everything else—dogged
persistence, bold ambition, and endless pluck. But it soon
became clear that as a team in the kitchen, Mom and Sharon
just jibed. Mom's decades of experience and practicality
coupled with Sharon's perfectionism and knowledge of seasonal ingredients and global flavors produced inspired results. They were learning from each other and loving it, and
I was soaking up a good bit by listening and observing. But I
mostly stayed at the periphery, dicing onions and arranging
cheese boards while drinking a glass of wine as they took on
the heavy-duty cooking. There was an unspoken ranking,
and I was on the bottom rung, the least experienced and
knowledgeable, always deferring to their expertise. In the
family kitchen, I regressed.

When it came to conceptualizing a meal, again I faded
into the background. Perhaps there'd be a few pints of languishing blueberries on the counter and wilting fresh thyme
in the produce drawer. Mom would petition for a blueberry
compote with balsamic and thyme. We'd put spoonfuls on
toast rounds topped with goat cheese, a great appetizer for
that night. Sharon would suggest the best use would be blueberry waffles with thyme-infused maple syrup for breakfast
the next morning. I didn't bother to interject; at that time
their ideas were far beyond my imagination. At home, I was

in the driver's seat, but in the family system, I complimented each idea, brokered an agreement, and awaited my minimal instructions.

This could have been ripe territory for sibling rivalry, but Sharon's superiority in the kitchen didn't trouble me. I had many things with Mom, but this was hers.

Funnily enough, while I may have been the least experienced cook in my family, in my circle of friends I was known as *the* cook. Like hearing your child's teacher describe a totally different person from the one you experience at home, my family would have thought, "Are we talking about the same person?" if they heard my friends describe my cooking. I threw together simple pots of soup for impromptu suppers and made killer crab cakes for cocktail parties. I baked elaborate cakes for birthday celebrations and catered friends' baby showers on my own. Out from under the shadow of Sharon and Mom, my culinary light shone bright.

It was on a weeklong sailing trip with a group of friends, adrift in the Atlantic Ocean, far from home, that I realized just how far I had come as a cook. The group assumed we would moor up and eat out most nights, but I offered to cook not only to save on cost but also to rescue us from a week of mediocre restaurant food. I made beans or eggs on toast for breakfast and laid out deli meat, bread, cheese, and chips for lunch, but it was dinner that I loved to make most. I relished the challenge of creating something special for eight people in a galley kitchen with very few ingredients and virtually no utensils or appliances.

I made shrimp tacos, burgers, Bolognese, and big salads, but my crowning glory was the last full day of our trip when the guys found a coconut on a deserted island. With little else to do, they spent nearly an hour trying to open it by smashing it with rocks, dropping it on boulders, and gouging it with any sharp object they could find. The coconut finally gave in. Elated with their accomplishment, they jokingly asked if I could incorporate the coconut into dinner. Bold with the constant compliments and cooking swagger I'd accrued during that week, I said "Sure," and my tone implied, "No big thing."

We returned to the boat and I looked at our stores. We had a whole chicken in the fridge, some spices I'd picked up at port, a sack of local onions, and a big bag of rice. I saw coconut chicken curry. On my own, I had room for the vision.

I butterflied the chicken and rubbed it down with a paste of oil, curry powder, cayenne, salt, and pepper. My friend lit the grill attached to the back of the boat and threw the chicken on. When the chicken started sticking, I didn't miss a beat, and I was back there with a metal spatula levering it off and flipping it over in a single swift move. I remember thinking: *If Mom and Sharon were here I would not be doing this. They would.*

I cracked the coconut into manageable pieces and grated the meat with the chintzy Dollar Store box grater. While dicing the onions with a dull knife, I had visions of Mom cooking in small, ill-equipped vacation rental kitchens in Maine and Nova Scotia. When the chicken came off the grill I let it rest to allow the juices to pool before pouring them into the simmering pot of stew that sat on the tiny stove next to a large pot of rice. Once I had shredded the chicken, I added the coconut meat to the sauce and let it simmer and reduce. One taste and I knew I had created something special.

As we dined on the back of the boat that night, my friends were so forthcoming with compliments that I had a pink-cheeked glow all evening. The kudos lasted throughout the meal and for days after. To this day they *still* talk about that dish: "The best curry we've ever had!" and "To think it was made on a little boat without so much as a trip to the grocery store!"

It was there, in the galley of a boat, without anyone to save me, that I found my culinary sea legs. I realized that I wasn't just a good cook; I was actually a great cook.

Not long after that trip, the family was together in Connecticut preparing Dad's birthday dinner. I had decided my contribution would be fresh Asian summer rolls, a way to demonstrate a skill I'd been perfecting.

I prepped the ingredients for the summer rolls, setting up bowls of julienned vegetables, vermicelli noodles, sliced scallions, avocado, and deep piles of lettuce, cilantro, and mint. Using my pointer finger as a thermometer, I heated the water to the temperature I had learned was just right and set to work, deftly soaking the rice paper for the correct amount of time, then layering it with filling, folding in the corners and rolling it up like a skinny little burrito. Sharon and Mom carried on forming crab cakes and knotting up homemade pretzels, occasionally glancing in my direction for signs of trouble, ready to step in and rescue a summer roll with a ripped skin or a rice paper stuck to the cutting board. But within a few minutes, I had five down without incident.

"Wow," Sharon said, "you're really good at that!"

Not wanting to break my concentration, I mumbled a quick, "Really? Thanks."

"Yeah." I could hear the slight edge of incredulity in her voice as she continued, "you're *nailing* this. I'm terrible at rolling those, Anthony just laughs at me. Seriously, that wet rice paper is a bitch to work with."

As my granny always says, if there had been buttons on my top they would have popped off. To have Mom, and particularly Sharon, impressed with a skill that I had was an important moment for me. I didn't make much of it. I just smiled as my family praised the summer rolls with peanut dipping sauce and blushed— same as on the boat—when they oohed and ahhed. And that was enough.

Every cook has a different path to the kitchen. For me, it took leaving the family circle to find my way in. I continue to improve as a cook each time I find myself challenged and without Mom and Sharon around. Family systems being what they are, I'll probably always be the third cook in our family kitchen, but that's okay.

When I have a child, I am going to call him into the kitchen one day when he is about eight years old, and I will show him how to undress a chicken from its skin. Unlike me he'll probably say, "Let *me* do it!" But if he rolls his eyes and asks, "Can I leave now?" I will know that a cook's education has just begun even if he doesn't know it.

Chicken Vindaloo

SERVES 8

Aside from opening a jar of premade sauce, curry doesn't get much easier than this, and the flavor is magnificent. Unlike the dish I made on the boat, you don't need a fresh coconut for this recipe—a jar or two of coconut milk will do. This Goan dish is traditionally made with mustard seeds and red wine vinegar, but we take a good shortcut by using whole grain mustard. One bite and we all said we could eat it again, and again, and again. And we have. Serve this flavorful stew over rice.

6 tablespoons grainy mustard

4 teaspoons ground cumin

4 teaspoons turmeric

1 1/2 teaspoons cayenne pepper

2 tablespoons red wine vinegar

4 pounds boneless, skinless chicken thighs, cut into 1-inch cubes

4 tablespoons vegetable oil, divided

Salt and ground black pepper

1 large sweet onion, cut into medium dice

12 to 15 garlic cloves, minced

2 cans (13.5 ounces each) regular (not light) coconut milk

Mix mustard, spices, and vinegar; set aside. Heat a large, wide pot over medium-high heat. Toss chicken with 2 tablespoons of the oil and sprinkle generously with salt and pepper; toss to coat. Working in batches to avoid overcrowding, sear chicken cubes until well browned, about 5 minutes per batch. Transfer to a plate. Add remaining 2 tablespoons of oil to the pot. Add onions and cook until softened, 4 to 5 minutes. Add garlic; sauté until fragrant, about a minute. Add mustard mixture; sauté until fragrant, about a minute longer. Add chicken, along with coconut milk and enough water (about 1 cup) to just cover the chicken. Bring to a simmer; reduce heat to medium-low and continue to simmer, partially covered, until flavors blend, about 45 minutes.

3.

A Cooking Lesson
in the Driveway

sharon

"YOU ARE SO MUCH LIKE YOUR MOTHER!" THOSE SEVEN LIT-
tle words are rarely a compliment for a twenty-
something woman, or any woman, for that matter.

When my husband tells me, as I eschew keyboard short-
cuts or struggle to grasp simple technological concepts, that
I am "pulling a Pam," I can only smile sheepishly. When I
find myself telling the long version of a short story, and
Maggy says, "Get to the point, *Mom*," I can't argue with the
truth. Protest is futile. I know I've already got a lot of my
mom in me, and if prevailing wisdom is to be believed I will
only become more like her as I age.

Along with her dubious technology skills and long-winded
storytelling, I've definitely inherited Mom's fierce loyalty, her
compassionate (though sometimes brutal) honesty, and her
bawdy sense of humor. I got her faith and her big heart for
people, too. But more than anything, I share her love of food.

I was always curious about what Mom was doing in the kitchen. She didn't cook like other mothers did. She didn't wear an apron, she didn't move daintily around the kitchen preparing just enough for four, she didn't do the dishes as she went along. The only word to describe her presence in the kitchen is *powerful*. She was fast—sometimes exacting and precise, other times quick and dirty. She could churn out hundreds of cookies, dozens of pies, or pounds of stir-fry during the hours we were at school. She could lift vats of soup and wrestle sacks of flour that weighed more than we did. She could break down a whole chicken (with a cordless phone tucked between her cheek and shoulder) faster than Maggy and I could peel four potatoes.

Mom was smart, perceptive, and thoughtful about her food. And she was absolutely unapologetic. When I'd eat over at friends' houses, their mothers would carefully inquire if the food was all right and make timorous excuses if it wasn't up to snuff. Not my mom. If dinner didn't turn out well, she served it anyway. If we didn't like it, she inquired as to why but never cowered under our criticism and certainly never allowed us to eat something else.

Yes, Mom was an absolute fiend in the kitchen. But she was gentle and elegant in her domain, too. She moved through the space like she owned it, juggling knives, spatulas, skillets, and mixing bowls with ease and grace. The whole kitchen might look like you should be wearing a hazmat suit, but there would always be a small oasis cleared on the kitchen island with two beautifully prepared and plated snacks—warm baguette with a few squares of dark chocolate and sliced fresh peaches or strawberries waiting to be dipped in plain yogurt and brown sugar—waiting for us when we got home from school. Mom would stop everything, wipe her hands, lean her forearms on the counter, and grin at us while we ate and chattered about our day. I'll always have that image of her seared into my memory—her skin a little dewy from exertion, her cheeks slightly flushed, kitchen towel thrown over her shoulder, a fresh burn blazing across her thumb. She was stunning.

During our growing-up years, I think Maggy spent her days in the kitchen because that's simply where Mom was. But it was more than the promise of munchies or motherly advice that drew me there. Mom noticed my little glowing ember of culinary interest and fanned it into a flame—though, doubtless, her fanning was done in the hope of cheap labor.

When I was in elementary school and Mom was in her *Cook's Illustrated* phase of relentless testing, she would pay me five dollars an hour to pull down all of her cookbooks (we're talking hundreds) and search the contents for whichever recipe was in her crosshairs. I would mark every chocolate cake (or lasagna or meatloaf) recipe in every cookbook, then I would load them into my little red wagon and pull them across the parking lot to Dad's office at church to photocopy, staple, and label each one.

Once I had dragged all the books back and put them away, I'd plunk down with Mom at our kitchen table and watch as she deconstructed each recipe in order to understand what made it work (or fail). She would tape sheets of legal paper to the sliding glass door in our family room and make vast charts that tracked every recipe and every ingredient—

sugar, all-purpose flour, cake flour, butter, shortening, cocoa, and so on. And then she would cook. Oh, would she cook.

She slogged through every single recipe—tasting, evaluating, and making notes. And she'd ask for my thoughts. Too dense, too light, too dry, good flavor, nice crumb? Then she would narrow down the variables and start testing her own variations. It went on like this for most of my childhood. It always started out fun, but after tasting literally forty-eight iterations of a dish, it was hard to like it at all much less determine whether Mom had finally nailed it. It took me years to eat chocolate cake again after she had perfected it. I still avoid roast turkey, even at Thanksgiving—much to everyone's holiday horror. And I am almost positive that I have not had chicken potpie since the night Mom served us version number twenty-six: the blue ribbon winner.

The first thing everyone always says when they find out who my mom is and what she does is: "Oh my gosh—you must have had the most amazing meals in your house!" And we did . . . sometimes. I always have to explain the unenviable part about being a guinea pig for cooking experiments. The worst part, though, was that Mom couldn't stand to throw away food. So the dry, flavorless pork (version three) we had for dinner on Monday night was often waiting to greet me when I opened my lunchbox on Tuesday afternoon. Sometimes on Wednesday, Thursday, and Friday, too.

For better or worse, this approach to cooking shaped me and my understanding of food. Mom always encouraged me to ask questions and then made time to answer them. She explained the role of fat in piecrust, the importance of protein in bread flour, the difference between baking soda and powder, the role of acid in marinades. She wanted me to *understand* cooking, not just enjoy it. Mom knew that great recipes are neither random nor the result of simple trial and error. Recipes work because there is science behind them, and knowing that science helps you to build better food and do so more efficiently.

However, Mom also taught me that perfection is an utterly subjective endeavor and that recipes work because there is room for imagination and experimentation, because they are full of passion and memory. I loved that she wasn't held captive by that careful, calculated approach to food; on any given night Mom could wing it with the best of 'em. When we'd go on vacation, our family would spend the morning hiking or sightseeing, but we almost always passed our afternoons roaming through tiny grocery stores, huge outdoor markets, dusty specialty shops, and local butchers, bakeries, and fishmongers. Mom would chat with the owners, ask what was good, and make her selections. We'd come home with bags full of whatever was freshest, prettiest, or most enthusiastically recommended, and then she'd just figure something out.

My mother's intelligent and thoughtful approach to food coupled with the wild creativity of making something entirely new grabbed hold of my guts. It thrilled me. I knew I wanted to be able to develop perfect recipes through careful experimentation, but I also knew that I wanted to be able to survey a countertop full of random ingredients and dream up dinner. In short, I wanted to be like my mother.

Over the years, I have developed both my skills and my passion for cooking. I'm a perfectionist by nature, so it wasn't a huge leap for me to embrace and cultivate my mom's scientific and calculating kitchen persona.

One night at a party, I found myself offering to bake a friend's wedding cake. Never mind that I'd never made a wedding cake or that they'd requested carrot cake and I didn't have a good recipe. With the courage only a few glasses of wine can bestow, I assured the happy couple that it would be great. The morning after, though, I woke up nursing a bit of a hangover and some serious insecurity. Could I really do this? Messing it up didn't just mean serving sad, deflated cake to my friends. It meant serving 200 people a crappy *wedding* cake! I considered backing out, but instead took a page out of my mom's book: I shelved the fear, threw a kitchen towel over my shoulder, and got to work.

My first instinct was, of course, to visit her section of my bookshelf. But I knew my mother's entire "perfect" repertoire of vigorously tested no-fail dishes, and carrot cake wasn't one of them.

So I combed the rest of my cookbooks and scoured the Internet for recipes and inspiration. I had no idea there were so many variables in carrot cake: coconut, pineapple, raisins, spices, nuts, buttermilk. I decided to stay classic (no canned crushed pineapple!) and I narrowed it down to a list of recipes that looked good and came from trustworthy sources. I baked each one exactly as directed to figure out which I liked best. In the ensuing weeks, I forced carrot cake on all our friends and coworkers, hounding them for opinions and feedback. Raisins or dried cranberries? Carrots too stringy? More spices or fewer? Walnuts or pecans? Too sweet? Too wet? Too dry? Too dense? Each cake had good points, but no one single cake had it all. Baking and tasting, I figured out what I liked about each cake and combined them into one recipe. Then I tested my version a few more times, tweaking it as I went. When I was *almost* certain my recipe was perfect, I sent it to my mom for the ultimate test.

Mom didn't make me wait for her opinion, knowing her gold star held the power to reduce my anxiety about this entire project. God bless her, she bought the ingredients and made the cake the same day, calling me the minute she'd taken a bite to tell me that it was, indeed, the best carrot cake she'd ever had. I could hear the pride in her voice as she asked questions about my method and research and listened to my answers. At the end of the phone call, she inquired about my plans for assembling the three-tiered wedding cake. Was I going to use dowels to support the weight of the top layers? Did I have the right platter? How was I going to transport it? My brain hiccupped and went blank. I had been so focused on getting the recipe right that I hadn't even considered the problem of stacking, frosting, decorating, and— horror of horrors—*moving* it to the event space!

On the big day, with the help of Google, YouTube videos, and a small army of friends, the cake was beautiful and, more important, delicious. Although I had to warn the couple to cut gingerly so as not to topple the precariously stacked layers, the cake remained in one piece until it was cut into 200. After the cake was mauled by enthusiastic guests and I no longer needed to worry about texture, taste, or structural integrity, I was ecstatic. I ate, drank, and danced, buoyed by this incredible feeling of pride and empowerment that had lodged itself in my chest. If I could make a wedding cake from scratch, I told myself, I truly could do *anything*.

While it's painfully obvious that I've inherited this recipe-testing, perfection-seeking style from my mother, I'm happy to report that I've got some of her resourceful, seat-of-your-pants cook in me, too. I can't seem to ignore the siren call of a farmers' market or local shop. Our little blue Honda needs a bumper sticker that warns, "This car brakes for produce," because Anthony and I are famous for pulling illegal U-turns for fresh eggs, farm stands, and hole-in-the-wall markets. And, since we hate to waste food just as much as Mom does, we've gotten good at creating tasty, albeit occasionally odd, meals with our local loot.

In my nearly thirty years of cooking, I have learned a lot from my mother, but I have yet to master all her skills. Though she's a total culinary rock star, Mom has an impossibly relaxed presence in the kitchen that doesn't intimidate people. I've always watched in wonder as her warmth invites people into the kitchen and her laissez-faire attitude encourages participation.

One summer when we were kids—I was maybe four and Maggy six—Mom was getting ready for a dinner party. It was, as I recall, ninety degrees, eighty percent humidity, and we were tugging on the hem of her shirt in our unair-conditioned kitchen taking turns whining, "Moooooommm, can we help?! We want to dooooooo something." In a completely classic move, Mom didn't yell at us, say no, or send us off to watch TV. She handed us a big bowl, a couple wooden spoons, and told us to grab ingredients out of the cupboard and go make something.

Bear-hugging all manner of jars and canisters, we toddled out to the driveway—which seemed as good a place as any—to create. As fading memory serves me, those cookies had only two ingredients: shredded coconut and rainbow sprinkles. Surely we put something else in there, but I have no idea what it was. I don't even remember if we baked them.

When with hyper-extended little arms we proudly presented Mom with our coconut sprinkle cookies—bits of grass, gravel, and rainbow-colored toppings be damned—she served them at her dinner party. I don't think I've ever felt that important, before or since. (Not even with the wedding cake.) The cookies were a hit! Who knows if they were accidentally delicious, decently edible, or if they ended up in the bathroom trash can tucked in cocktail napkins. But everyone had a great time telling us that they were good and laying those "Mmm" noises on thick.

Serving coconut sprinkle cookies next to her carefully prepared dinner is *so* Mom—a remarkable combination of perfectionist and perfection-less.

Over the years we've loved to tease Mom about her kitchen mantra. If the yogurt's got a little blue fuzz around the top, just scrape it off and "it's fine." If you've accidentally diced the bell peppers instead of slicing them, don't worry, "it's fine." If you burned the bread, undercooked the pasta, overworked the pie dough, or put Palmolive instead of Cascade in the dishwasher: "S'fine." There is something so incredibly hospitable about Mom's "It's fine" attitude. Guests who volunteer to help aren't worried that they're mincing the garlic wrong in the great Pam Anderson's kitchen—they're just drinking their wine, telling stories, working the knife, and having a good time. It's pretty amazing to watch.

I've always wondered how Mom's incredible kitchen savvy can be paired with such abounding culinary mercy. This seemingly impossible combination makes people around her *want* to cook and—better yet—believe they can.

Of all the things I could have learned from my mother, I wish I had studied and practiced this kind of grace. The truth is, I just don't have it. I wish I didn't care if the peppers got diced instead of sliced, but I do. I wish I could be better at letting undercooked pasta and overworked dough slide, but I'm not. Most of all, I wish I didn't hesitate when people wander into my kitchen and ask if they can help. The truth is, I can't abide mistakes because I still haven't figured out how *not* to give a shit when my food flops.

Though my mother's identity is certainly wrapped up in cooking and feeding people, unlike me, Mom has long since figured out how to separate each dish from her identity and self-worth. If her cake falls, she is not a failure. If someone doesn't like her food, it's not personal. Though I've spent decades shadowing my mom in the kitchen, it's clear there is still much I need to learn.

And so it would seem, the joke's on this twenty-something woman. Because I could only *wish* to be more like my mother.

Perfect Carrot Cake

This is the cake recipe I so painstakingly developed for my friends' wedding. The cake technique is based on Greg Case's version, but with many of my own twists and additions. To me, this recipe is perfect, but feel free to fiddle with the spices and use raisins instead of dried cranberries or walnuts instead of pecans. When making the frosting, be sure to leave the cream cheese and butter out on the counter for at least 4 hours (and longer if you can!)—it is the only foolproof way to achieve a smooth, creamy, and impossibly light cream cheese frosting.

For the cake:

1 pound carrots, peeled and cut into 1-inch pieces

2 cups (10 ounces) all-purpose flour

2 teaspoons baking soda

1 teaspoon table salt

1 teaspoon ground cinnamon

1/2 teaspoon ground nutmeg

1/2 teaspoon ground ginger

1/4 teaspoon ground allspice

1/4 teaspoon ground cloves

3/4 cup dried cranberries, coarsely chopped

3/4 cup pecans, toasted and coarsely chopped

4 large eggs

continued on next page

1 cup granulated sugar

1 cup packed dark brown sugar

1 1/4 cup vegetable oil

For the frosting:

2 packages (8 ounces each) cream cheese, at room temperature

2 sticks (16 tablespoons) unsalted butter, at room temperature

4 teaspoons vanilla extract

1/4 teaspoon table salt, more to taste

2 to 3 cups confectioner's sugar (depending on your preference)

MAKE THE CAKE: Move the oven rack to middle position and heat the oven to 350°F. Line two 9-inch round cake pans with parchment, spray them with nonstick cooking spray, and dust with flour.

IN A FOOD PROCESSOR fitted with the steel blade, chop the carrots very finely to about the consistency of large couscous. Transfer carrots to a medium bowl and rinse the food processor bowl—you will need it again.

IN A LARGE BOWL, combine the flour, baking soda, salt, and spices. Whisk to blend thoroughly. Transfer 1/4 cup of this mixture to a small bowl, add the cranberries and pecans, and toss to combine.

IN THE FOOD PROCESSOR fitted again with the steel blade, mix the eggs and sugars until thoroughly combined. With the machine running, slowly add the oil in a steady stream until well blended. Using a silicone spatula, scrape the egg mixture into the dry ingredients and stir gently to combine. Add the carrots and the cranberry/nut mixture; stir to combine.

DIVIDE THE BATTER evenly between the prepared pans. Bake until a toothpick inserted in the center of each cake comes out clean, 40 to 45 minutes. Let the pans cool on a rack to room temperature before inverting them to remove the cakes. Allow cakes to cool completely before frosting.

MAKE THE FROSTING: In a stand mixer fitted with the whisk attachment (or using a hand mixer), whip together the cream cheese and butter. Add the vanilla and salt. One cup at a time, add the confectioner's sugar until you reach your desired sweetness, and continue whipping until the frosting is light and airy.

ASSEMBLE THE CAKE: Put a small dollop of icing in the center of a large, flat serving plate (this helps glue the cake to the plate). Place one cake upside down on the plate. Using a butter knife or offset metal spatula, evenly spread about 1 cup of the frosting over the top of the first cake. Top with the remaining cake layer, right side up. Spread the entire cake with the remaining frosting and refrigerate until ready to serve.

4.

The Making of a Mom

pam

'LL ADMIT IT. WHEN THE GIRLS WERE BABIES AND TODDLERS, I WAS
an okay mom. Not Mother of the Year. Barely twenty-six
when Maggy was born and just nine days past my twenty-
eighth birthday when Sharon entered the world, I was still
so busy figuring out my life, I didn't have time for hours of
block play on the floor and endless rounds of peekaboo.

During Maggy's and Sharon's early years I was strad-
dling two jobs. A traveling property adjustor for an insurance
company by day, I got a respectable salary, a company car, a
flexible schedule, and health-care coverage for us all. As caterers on nights and weekends, David and I made the nice
chunks that went toward grad school tuition, family recre-
ation, and home renovation.

Not knowing I was early-stage pregnant with Maggy, I
changed insurance jobs. (Even the doc's test was negative, so
how was I to know?) To try to make up for my honest mis-
take of starting a new job three months pregnant I raced

back to work just six weeks after she was born. A little over a year later I was pregnant with Sharon. Having her so quickly on the heels of Maggy (that and all the company time spent catering on the sly) I felt such guilt that I took a mere four weeks off with her. I had no patience for the pump. After a few weeks I figured a little of Mom's milk was better than none. I stuffed nursing pads down my shirt, quickly dried up, and moved on.

I don't think it would have been so easy for me to walk out the door every morning if David hadn't been such a big part of our childcare solution. Though we never formally discussed it, he and I traded places. David is clearly masculine—loves sports, beer, and his chain saw—but early on he was the one who mother-loved Maggy and Sharon. Whenever he wasn't in class or teaching, he was with them.

I, on the other hand, was an ambitious unformed Southern girl, finding her way. Finally let loose in the world, I was passionate, with a lot to prove. While I headed off to work each day, David lovingly spooned purees into Maggy's and Sharon's hungry mouths, cradled them before naps, and held them tight when they weren't happy. Given our traditional upbringing, this role reversal stretched and deepened us both. Of course I cared for the girls—I loved making their food and treasured our nighttime rituals—but on the whole, I didn't find babies all that interesting.

I think I was meant to be a papoose mother, a woman who carries her baby on her back, the way those strong and beautiful African women carry their babies in a sling behind them. It's a "hands-free" method so the woman can do her work. It's "take your daughter to work," every day. I've seen plenty of American mothers with babies in slings, but they're always in front, at the center of the mother's gaze. That's not me. I'm a sling-the-kid-behind-me mom, so I can get on with my work.

Unfortunately, it wasn't acceptable to show up at my office with a baby slung to my back. But nights and weekends, I took my daughters to work—in the kitchen. Maggy and Sharon spent more time there than anywhere else in our home. As babies they stayed near the action, alternating between their carriers propped on the countertop and the nearby swing. Once they could scoot around, the rolling walker was their third kitchen habitat. As toddlers they advanced to sitting on the counter, dangling their feet as I stuffed snow peas and cherry tomatoes. When they were old enough to help, they stood on a sturdy kitchen chair. I suppose I should have sympathized the day Sharon scraped her little thumb on a vegetable peeler. Instead, I told her I was proud of her first war wound and showed her ten or fifteen of my own kitchen scars.

Cooking and working, pursuing dreams and juggling kids and jobs—this is how our family life ticked along, until the Tuesday after Labor Day in September 1990 when both girls headed off to school. It was Sharon's first day of kindergarten, Maggy started second grade, and I hopped a train for New York City. *Cook's* magazine had folded and I was now the food editor at *Restaurant Business* magazine. My old job at *Cook's* had been kitchen and recipe centered. This job offered new challenges of writing, reporting, and managing a food section. I sighed with relief because finally, finally we were done piecemealing childcare. Maggy and Sharon were both officially in school, and David and I were free to climb as far as we could, he in his world and I in mine.

What I did not anticipate was how this job shift would impact our family. Working two jobs in the past, I had proved I could endure hard labor and long hours, but I had never worked such a relentlessly inflexible job so far from home. I'd head for the train station at seven-thirty in the morning and not return until nearly seven at night, on top of which there were late-night press events and days and days of travel.

And this was just *my* life. On the mornings he had early meetings, David dropped off the girls with another clergy couple who lived on the church campus where they'd stay until the bus arrived. An afterschool nanny was with them until David got home, and he was usually out the door going to night meetings thirty minutes after I walked in. As the youth minister he worked most weekends, and of course around Christmas and Easter he disappeared for days.

Maybe I would have had a stronger stomach for this life if just once in a while I could have sneaked away from work for Sharon's afterschool Brownie program or had a leisurely afternoon to help Maggy with her penguin project. The few times I got the call that my child was sick I was helpless. An hour and a half away, going home was not an option. David would have to rearrange his schedule and handle it. The girls wanted to take piano lessons. With David at work and me in the city, who would take them? Who would make them practice? Having both kids in school was supposed to mean the parents were free. So we thought.

A year in, our family was starting to tank. The kids were acting out with the nanny, and there were quiet concerns at school. When I made legitimate time demands on David— "You've been on a youth group retreat all weekend, and I head back to work tomorrow. You need to get your ass home for Sunday supper with your family"—he'd defiantly meander across the parking lot toward home in his own sweet time. His actions were telling. I knew he didn't love me very much then. The feeling was mutual. I wasn't crazy about him either.

I was starting to believe we'd become one of those divorce statistics. I didn't want this for our family, but I didn't see a way forward either. Late one spring night as I was coming home on the train, it occurred me. I finally realized I did have a choice. I could keep climbing the culinary ladder and risk breaking up our family, or I could quit and stay home. Maybe it was finally time for me to mother love.

The still-small voice grew louder and more intense. At the end of the school year, I gave my notice. As Sharon and Maggy hopped off the bus that last day of school, I was there waiting for them. Our first summer together I felt like Maria with my two little von Trapp girls. We went strawberry picking, ran under the sprinkler, spent afternoons at the beach, sneaked off to matinees. Finally there was some peekaboo time in our lives, and I delighted in it. So did Maggy and Sharon. They kept telling me how great it was to have me home. The starving maternal side of my soul soaked up the mommy praise, but the realistic side thought, "Hah— they'll get over it and quickly take me for granted." But they never did, really. I was finding my mother love and it showed no sign of abating.

That summer David and I were coming up on year four- teen, and it felt like the year to renew our commitment. I bought new dresses for the girls and me and ordered bou- quets from the florist. On a hot Sunday afternoon in June the four of us walked to Saint Luke's Chapel, and with Maggy and Sharon as our witnesses and the Reverend Ann Kimball as our officiant, David and I renewed our wedding vows.

Maggy and Sharon were intrigued by the ceremony— this was a mini wedding after all—but on some level I think they understood that this was not merely a sentimental act. This was their mother and father's attempt to keep the fam- ily intact. After the ceremony, Chuck's Steakhouse was the site of our cautious celebration. David and I were far from full reconciliation, but we had done what we could to right this ship.

You'd have thought the financial stress of trying to sur- vive on one very modest clergy salary in a wealthy town would have been overwhelming. Quite the opposite. The year I worked in New York I had never made more money and never felt poorer in my life. There were transportation costs and the nanny. Clothes, and lots of them. We ate out, relied on pricey convenience foods, and spent lots on stuff to soothe our fretting spirits.

In contrast, the year I stayed home there was finally time for leisurely fun. Instead of dinner on the fly we made pots of long-simmering soup. We shopped at secondhand stores, went for long walks, and read lots—*The Chronicles of Narnia*, *Lord of the Rings*, *Watership Down*, *The Hobbit*, anything by Madeleine L'Engle. That Halloween we set up a haunted house in the abandoned stone barn on our property and invited the whole costumed neighborhood.

Was it just my perception or did David have more time now, too? That December I bought thick, rich jewel-toned construction paper and the four of us spent hours after dinner eating popcorn, drinking hot chocolate, and making a paper chain. David got on a ladder and hung it all around the living room with masking tape and thumbtacks. The swooping boughs of colorful scalloping transformed our home into a Nutcracker fantasy—a dream we all helped to create.

We gently laid the chain in huge boxes for storage, and for years we'd pull it out and hang it with all the other Christmas decorations. The chain was made of good paper and held up well. Even after the girls had outgrown something so juvenile we held on to that chain for years. We didn't hang it, but we couldn't throw away the project that symbolized our togetherness as a family. For the first time in my life I understood: Success and money can't buy happiness. Really.

I had no idea that in giving up my career for my girls, I'd get it all back in a have-my-cake-and-eat-it-too sort of way. Six months after I left my job, my old publisher at *Cook's* magazine, Chris Kimball, called and gave me the chance to cook, write, and edit from home. I could do the work I loved and never leave the home and family for whom I was now mother.

For the next decade the girls had front-row seats at my job. As they left for school I was already setting out bowls, measuring ingredients, and getting ready for the day's tests. When they came home, I had finished dishes for them to taste and evaluate. Sometimes it was fun, like the brownie tastings. Other times, not so much. Like the time I enlisted them to detect and register the fine nuances of sweet potato casserole crumble.

They caught the bug early. It was on one of our Maine vacations that they came into their own as cooks. Inspired by an episode of *Ramona*, in which eight-year-old Ramona Quimby makes a crazy but tasty dinner for her family from a package of chicken legs and a carton of orange yogurt, eight-year-old Sharon and ten-year-old Maggy pleaded to make dinner for David and me one night. What a lovely thing, I thought. I'd help plan the menu and supervise the process, helping as needed. This, however, was not their vision. They wanted to look in our fridge, make something up, and surprise us. *And* they wanted us out of the house.

As Sharon and Maggy embarked on their first culinary adventure, David and I sat on the deck with our backs to the large kitchen picture window, nervously sipping gin and tonics, ready to first-respond if one of them sliced a thumb, burned a finger, or set the place on fire. Every time we turned our heads to check on our little chefs, we'd get a finger wagging. Like little *Top Chef* contenders, they diced and sliced, grated and sautéed their way to a tasty little taco supper. It was a proud night for us all, and each year from then on the girls carried on the vacation dinner tradition.

I had no idea how empowering Maggy and Sharon in the

cooking at such an early age would so profoundly impact me. Eventually, I would need their help in the kitchen.

It was June 2009. I had just turned in the manuscript for *Perfect One-Dish Dinners* and was feeling both relief that my sixth book was in the birth canal and anxiety that the comfortable, familiar world I had known as a cookbook author was rapidly changing.

The 2008 economic crisis had accelerated the paradigm shift in the publishing world. My formula for selling cookbooks that had worked so well for the last decade was becoming obsolete. Food editor friends at magazines and newspapers were losing their jobs, and cookbook editor colleagues were being dismissed. All across the country, cooking class sales were stale. QVC was drying up. A new way was emerging, and blogging was hot.

Sharon, now a web editor at *Fine Cooking* magazine, and Maggy, budding foodie and social media whiz, understood the new reality. Both told me emphatically that without a digital platform I was dead. I knew they were right, and with the book off to the publisher, I was ready to move. It just so happened that my readiness and their eagerness coincided with a family vacation to Florida.

The paradigm of our mother-daughter relationship was shifting, too. There had been the long tradition of Sharon and Maggy cooking a dinner on vacation, but this year it wasn't a kiddie show. Savvy young women now, Sharon and Maggy each offered to take charge of one of the dinners. Maggy suggested a tandoori mixed grill she had seen on a recent blog. Sharon had a marinated skirt steak recipe from *Fine Cooking* she wanted us to try. And when it came time to shop, they weren't just along for the ride. We all went to the supermarket together, as women. At the liquor store, they suggested wine pairings and cocktails perfect for a summer's night in Florida.

In years past I had happily shared my kitchen for a night, but this vacation the girls were setting up shop as my peers, and I was equal parts delighted and threatened. I led with excitement and openness to their new ideas and recipes, and I loved the new energy, creativity, and flavors they were bringing to the table, but a tiny piece of me liked the days when I ruled in the kitchen.

Fortunately my openness and gratitude outweighed my apprehension, and it paid off in a way I never could have anticipated. That week, as we explored our newfound kitchen roles, sunned on the beach, and took long walks, Sharon and Maggy were also my guides as I contemplated a new online venture.

Without help I couldn't make it in the digital world. I knew that. With the kind of parental wisdom that comes to adult children, they knew it, too. Somehow as we walked along the ocean and dreamed of what this blog could be, we were all three in this virtual kitchen. As we free-associated names under that hot Florida sun, I blurted out, "Too Many Cooks!" I'm not sure which one of us said it next, but we all knew it was right. I wasn't alone in the kitchen anymore. We were "Three Many Cooks."

Sometimes I catch myself wondering: Had I pursued my career with abandon, might I have made the culinary A-list? As I've watched some of my more ambitious peers fall and those ahead of me stumble, I think about the warning sign

I almost blew past nearly two decades ago. I'll still take success if it comes, and I'm not turning down anybody's money. But I'm not counting on that to make me happy. For that I'm hanging on to the best loves I've got—married love and mother love. And paper chains.

Quick Italian Wedding Soup

SERVES 6

After Sharon left home, I continued to show mother love by making her favorite dish her first night home. For years it's been chicken noodle soup, and Italian Wedding Soup is her new favorite iteration. Her last visit, I tried suggesting a new soup, but she wouldn't hear of it.

3/4 pound chicken Italian sausage,
    meat removed from casing

6 tablespoons dry bread crumbs

1 minced garlic clove

2 tablespoons grated Parmesan cheese

1 large egg

2 tablespoons olive oil

1 large onion, cut into medium dice

2 each: medium carrots and celery stalks, cut into
    medium dice

6 cups chicken broth

3/4 cup Israeli (or Middle Eastern) couscous

2 tablespoons chopped fresh dill

8 ounces (8 cups) baby spinach leaves

Salt and pepper

Mix sausage, bread crumbs, garlic, Parmesan, and egg. Divide mixture and shape into 24 meatballs. Heat oil in a large soup kettle. Add meatballs, in batches if necessary, and cook, turning only once, until well browned, about 5 minutes total. Remove from pan. Using additional oil if necessary, add onion, carrots, and celery; sauté until tender, about 5 minutes. Add broth and bring to a simmer. Add couscous and meatballs; cook to blend flavors, about 10 minutes. Add dill and spinach; cook until spinach wilts, a minute or so longer. Adjust seasonings, including salt and pepper to taste. Serve.

Bacon-Brussels Sprout Pizza

SERVES 4

Before Maggy dramatically curbed her red meat consumption, she craved lamb stew her first night home. These days it's always homemade pizza, and one of her favorite combos— David's, too—is bacon and Brussels sprouts. If you're watching calories or meat consumption, 6 ounces of bacon is very satisfying.

1/2 recipe Simple Pizza Dough *(page 61)*

6 to 8 ounces thick-cut bacon, cut into 1-inch pieces

2 cups trimmed and thinly sliced Brussels sprouts, about 1/2 pound

8 ounces smoked mozzarella, thinly sliced

Parmesan cheese

Prepare and stretch Simple Pizza Dough as directed (page 61). Adjust oven rack to lowest position and heat oven to 500°F.

Meanwhile, fry bacon in a large skillet over medium-high heat until partially rendered, 3 to 4 minutes. Remove with a slotted spoon and place on a paper towel–lined plate. Pour off all but 1 tablespoon of the bacon renderings and return skillet to burner. Add Brussels sprouts to empty skillet; stir-fry until just wilted, about a minute. Transfer to plate.

Top each of the 4 stretched pizza doughs with equal portions of cheese, then Brussels sprouts, and finally bacon.

Bake until crust is crisp and has darkened in color, about 12 minutes. Remove from oven; grate Parmesan over top and serve.

Simple Pizza Dough

**MAKES A SCANT 2 POUNDS
OR 8 SMALL PIZZAS**

1/2 cup warm water and 1 1/4 cup tap water

1 envelope active dry yeast (or a generous
  2 teaspoons)

2 tablespoons extra-virgin olive oil

4 cups bread flour

2 teaspoons table salt

cornmeal for the pan

Measure 1/2 cup warm water in a 2-cup measuring cup. Whisk yeast into water; let stand until it dissolves and expands, about 5 minutes. Measure in remaining 1 1/4 cups of water (for 1 3/4 cups total) and oil to yeast mixture. Meanwhile, pulse flour and salt in a large food processor fitted with a steel blade. Pour liquid ingredients over flour; pulse to form a rough soft ball. Continue to process until dough is smooth and satiny, about 30 seconds longer. Turn dough onto a floured work surface and knead a few seconds to form a smooth ball. Place in a vegetable cooking spray–coated bowl and cover with plastic wrap. Let rise to double in size, 2 to 3 hours.

continued on next page

Without punching it down, dump dough onto a lightly floured work surface. Using a chef's knife or a metal dough scraper, halve dough. Cut one half of the dough into quarters and stretch each piece into a 12 × 4-inch rectangle. Place them crosswise on a large cornmeal-coated baking sheet. Punch down remaining half and wrap and refrigerate or freeze for another time.

5.

The Blood of Sisters

maggy

THERE IS A PHOTO OF SHARON AND ME TAKEN AT A TRINITY Church Youth Group retreat around 1998 when I was fifteen and Sharon was thirteen. It's the kind of photo that lives in a shoe box and not on a shelf because it's an image I'd like to forget. I come across it perhaps once a year while looking for baby pictures or funny photos of Dad with mutton chops, and my instinct is always to keep flicking through. But I make myself stop for a minute and go back to that time.

My discomfort is twofold. This was the height of those awkward early teen years for both Sharon and me. I'm wearing baggy, wide-legged jeans, a button-down plaid shirt, a thick ball and chain necklace, and a ratty pair of Vans sneakers. I look guarded and self-conscious, a little overweight, with short, bleached hair. I'm eking out a half smile, but there is no light emanating from my face, no discernible joy in my aura. Sharon is next to me. We're close, but not touching. She's in a similar button-down shirt, Doc Marten shoes barely peeking out from underneath her own wide-leg jeans. She's even got the ball and chain necklace. Curly hair cut to the angle of her chin draws my eyes to her mouth and her own poor attempt at a smile, trying to cover a set of braces.

The other, more painful reason I hide this photo is because it reminds me how cruel I was to Sharon that year. She looked up to me, her big sister, wanted to do as I did, wear what I wore, and I made it exceedingly clear that I mostly wanted nothing to do with her. I was trying to break out and be my own person—this was also the year I changed the spelling of my name from "Maggie" to "Maggy" because there was another Maggie in the year below me. Clearly, I was going through some shit.

One look at this snapshot and it all floods back on me, how I made fun of her jeans, the exact same as my own. How I shunned her completely, banning her from hanging out with me and my friends, even when Mom appealed to me on her behalf. How I used her to help me with homework or to lie for me, all of which she did hoping for a little kindness in return, something I couldn't find in my teen-darkened heart to do. The person I am now looks back and feels sadness and shame that I could not have been kinder, more loving and gentle to my little sister.

The big-sis imitation phase didn't last long in part because it wasn't who Sharon really was and also because of the stress it was putting on our relationship. So she traded the ball and chain necklace and punk rock music for Lip Smackers gloss and boy bands. That eased the tension, and we entered a period of relative calm. And so it has continued over the years, oscillating between sworn enemies and bosom buddies.

When we fought as kids, it was hitting, pinching, and hair pulling, but when we got older it was verbal. We were sisters who shared *everything* in the good times, and so when trouble erupted, we knew how to inflict maximum damage, like a heat-seeking missile launched with insider intel. But even in those moments of hot-faced hate, we knew that it would never be more than a day before we were back to normal. What I've come to realize over the last thirty years is that Sharon and I are never going to have a lukewarm relationship. It will always be mercurial, hot or cold. We will never stop saying astonishingly hurtful things to each other, but we will never stop being something that I struggle to name, a relationship that goes beyond sisters or best friends.

The fine line between love and hate, intimacy and violence, is well known. The volatility of our relationship probably stemmed from the fact that we were so often together. The closeness of our family was sometimes parentally forced and at other times affectionately chosen. While our friends would spend whole weekends at their friends' houses, we were on a shorter leash. Mom and Dad must have figured that other parents would be less strict about where we went, who we hung out with, and what we watched, so we spent more time at home. Thus, Sharon and I were often obliged to be together—often bored—looking for something to do, the perfect conditions for a blowout fight.

When Granny and Papa would come to stay, Mom and Dad would sleep in my bedroom, giving them the master bedroom and bath. Sharon and I adored Granny and Papa too much to say goodnight, so we built a bed on the floor next to them.

One night during their holiday visit in 1991 (and no doubt after a prolonged period of family togetherness), Sharon and I got into a quiet fight: one of us wasn't respecting the "pillow line" that divided the makeshift bed in two. As we lay there in the dark, grandparents dozing off next to us, I shoved Sharon back across the line. She retaliated and we were off. I was bigger and stronger and pummeled her with closed-fist punches. In this asymmetrical war, Sharon resorted to hair pulling and pinching, all in the dark and silent room. Sharon finally yelped. Granny rolled over and turned on the light to see what was going on. Sharon's lower lip was quivering, her eyes were filled with tears, glistening in the low light. I'm sure I just looked guilty. We had both been inflicting pain, but even then I remember the feeling of knowing, like all bullies, that I had taken advantage of the weak.

Granny put a swift end to the war, and Sharon and I went to sleep. The next morning, she and I were up early, playing with our basket of Barbies and watching *Garfield* on the VCR in the family room as Mom and Granny fried up pattie sausages and stirred cheese grits. The night before was long forgotten.

We didn't have a choice. There was nowhere to go, no one else to play with. We had no cable. Smartphones had not been invented, and even if they had we would not have been allowed to have one. Sharon and I had to depend on each other for amusement. She and I built tree houses at every house we ever lived in, put on elaborate plays and fashion shows, and made music videos with a video camera that weighed thirty pounds. We created secret clubs in the attic and made cookies in the driveway. We played "school" and "bank" and read books side by side on the bed for hours on end.

We were forced together, but even when the opportunity arose to be apart—at bedtime—we wanted to be together. After our family left student housing at Yale Divinity School, Sharon and I had our own rooms but continued to sleep in the twin beds in Sharon's room. When I was old enough to think I *should* be sleeping on my own, I still wanted to be near Sharon. The same year as the nighttime fight incident, my Christmas list was simple (and poorly spelled):

Dear Santa,

For Christmas I want troll clothe, roller blaids, and a tunnel from Sharon's room to mine

Love,
Maggie Anderson

P.S. And a radio if you have time

I got the roller blades and some new clothes for my troll dolls, but the tunnel was not to be. That I had to construct in my imagination. Meanwhile, we carried on sleeping in the same room.

Despite all the rivalry, my love for my sister went instinctually deep. It wasn't just about having someone to play with or coordinating matching outfits. I was protective of her.

While on vacation in Maine one summer, Mom and Dad announced that they were sending us to sailing camp. Not art camp or writing camp or acting camp, or anything in which we had shown *actual* interest, but sailing camp. This was Maine, after all. When they broke the news, Sharon, who wrote the book on fear, started listing things that might lurk beneath the water. Sharks that bite, whales that tip over small boats, lobsters with claws that pinch. Her paranoia was infectious. I knew something of the icy waters that lapped the coast of Maine—even in August!—and started to worry about water so cold it made you stop breathing. We would have preferred to read *Boxcar Children* and *Nancy Drew* all day. What was meant to be a fun summer of sailing along Maine's jagged coastline was actually an anxiety-producing nightmare for both of us.

On the first day of sailing camp, our worst fears were realized. Before being given permission to come aboard, you had to prove that you could swim without a life jacket from the dock out to a boat anchored maybe a hundred feet away and then all the way back. I went first, wanting to prove to Sharon it would be okay. When I surfaced back at the dock, they told me I had broken a record, second only to an instructor's swim the previous year. I had done it, but remained afraid for my little sister. When I got out of the water, two other campers were waiting to wrap me in a towel and hustle me inside so I could change into dry clothes. No sooner had the towel gone over my shoulders than I started to cry. Sharon was up next. "My little sister!" I pleaded. "It's so cold. And that boat is so far. She's not going to make it!" They were moving me along and I couldn't stop. I was too scared for Sharon even to stay and watch. She was, of course, fine. In a matter of minutes we were huddling together for warmth, laughing in triumph. This remains my most powerful memory of sisterly love and protection.

We had become used to this closeness, this constant togetherness. It may have come with a certain (tolerable) level of dysfunction, but it worked. The relationship was inverse, illogical: The harder we fought, the deeper we loved.

By the time I went to college, everyone in the house, Sharon included, was ready for me to go. It had been a rough few years as I ran the gauntlet of my teens. While not entirely uncommon, the stress I put on the family system had been relentless and exhausting. The fall of 2001 and my freshman year at Kenyon College couldn't come soon enough. But the very minute their Ford Aerostar pulled away from campus, I felt drawn to be home, to come back to center.

Sharon and I missed each other more than we had anticipated and counted down the months, weeks, and days until we would be reunited for that first Thanksgiving break. Through our phone calls, texts, and emails, we saw clearly for the first time that food, which had always been a part of our lives, was really the thing we associated with home and togetherness. It was less what we would "do" when we were reunited, it was more what we would cook, eat, and drink as a family.

We passed the time apart by planning every minute detail of Thanksgiving dinner, Sharon perpetually concerned about just how many pans of stuffing Mom would make, while I petitioned for sweet potato casserole and bacon-wrapped Brussels sprouts. When we'd exhausted that conversation, we made the list of everything else we simply *needed* to do together: have breakfast at our favorite diner, strong-arm Mom into making lamb stew for dinner, visit the local bakery for apple cider doughnuts, and get everything bagel sandwiches loaded with scrambled eggs and sharp cheddar cheese. (We had far better metabolisms back then!) The most important was to make time for "coffee walks," where Sharon and I would wake at dawn, make a pot of coffee, fill travel mugs, head out for a walk, and talk for a couple hours before breakfast—uninterrupted sister time. If there was something important to talk about when I was home, that's when it would happen—new loves, fights with friends, questions about our future. When we got back, we'd bring in the *New York Times*, put on another pot of coffee, and set to making a batch of our favorite pumpkin scones for breakfast. It had become so—civilized.

There were moments when I thought our relationship had crossed into new, adult territory, a few tiffs here and there but safe from the previous wild mood swings. The relatively smooth cruising lasted a few years, but our relationship was never tested so deeply as the summer before I got married.

Sharon had just come back from her junior year abroad in Greece where she had enjoyed her first taste of real freedom outside the confines of the family home and the safety of Williams College. There had been Greek food to enjoy and booze to consume, and she had taken up serious smoking—a vice that had landed her in a Greek hospital for several days with a bout of pneumonia from which she had only just recovered. She had had the time of her life, but she was coming apart at the seams. Coming back home and trying to settle after a semester away, amid all the wedding drama, was nearly impossible. She was unmoored and confused. Making matters worse, the bridesmaid dress she had ordered while in Greece did not fit—something about measuring in metric and converting to inches. The entire summer she was just plain "hangry," while crash dieting to fit into that damn dress. To top it all off, she was in a relationship with a boy who was no good.

I, on the other hand, had been living at home that year, leveling out after college, learning and living an adult life grounded in routine, discipline, and moderation as I prepared to leave the family home for good. I had been going to the gym every morning, working a great nine to five, and planning a spectacular wedding to my wonderful fiancé whom everyone loved. We couldn't have been in more opposite places.

Sharon came home in the early summer as the wedding preparations reached a crescendo. Big decisions had been made, now it was down to the nitty-gritty. I'd had visions of Sharon and me holed up in my room for hours with Starbucks and a stack of wedding magazines looking for inspiration. In reality, conversations with my sister about the wedding went something like this:

"What kind of ribbon should we use to wrap the silverware?"

"I literally don't give a fuck."

Sure, the old sibling rivalry was at work, but it didn't take Freud to figure out that we were both anticipating acute separation anxiety. We had managed our separateness in the college years. It was a soft transition because our center, our home, was still the same—we had long breaks and endless summers to catch up. But I wasn't moving down the street or even a few states over. I was moving to England to be with my husband indefinitely. The center that held our fractious relationship in balance was slipping away. Without coffee walks and pumpkin scones, how would it work?

Sharon was the maid of honor at my wedding. Though she cared demonstrably little for ribbon, she carried out her other duties exceedingly well. With Mom, she planned a killer bachelorette party that included lobster, clams, corn, and a case of pink champagne on an island. She wrangled friends to help set up for the reception and did a better-than-professional job on my makeup for the wedding. But—not surprisingly—the most memorable thing she did was to give a speech and a toast that I don't think any of our guests have yet forgotten.

It started, "It would be the understatement of the century to say that this has been a rough summer for the Anderson family. I have never loved my sister so much and wanted to smack her upside the head so often as in the last two months." (Yes, that pretty well summed up the previous twenty-plus years.) She regaled the crowd with embarrassing stories of wedding stress, referencing, of course, the pathetic incident with the ribbon, edited for expletives. The conflict and warfare had been near-constant, but, she observed, it was ever thus. She'd even found evidence to back it up, little scraps of paper and other gems my parents had stuffed in my memorabilia box in the attic: two letters from our childhood, and that Christmas wish list from 1991.

The first letter was to Dad, dated April 1991, written in desperation from seven-year-old Sharon, pleading: "Dad, you have to *do something* about Maggie!" She couldn't take it anymore, her hideous sister always picking a fight. Nevertheless in the next letter, dated just four months later, the shoe was on the other foot.

"Dear Maggie, I'm sorry about reading your stories. I didn't mean to make you bleed. I won't read your things anymore. Please don't give me the silent treatment. I know you have the right to be mad, but please forgive me. From, Sharon."

It was all there in juvenile miniature, the tragicomedy of our sisterhood. The intense need for each other: the battles, the rupture, the plea for restoration. Even the blood. We have always drawn blood.

Having read my Dear Santa letter of 1991 earlier in her speech (wherein I requested the tunnel from my room to hers), Sharon ended her wedding speech with this:

Dear Santa,

This Christmas I want a new iPod, a graduate school education, and a tunnel from Darien, Connecticut, to Woking, England.

The crowd erupted into laughter and impassioned clapping, but no one outside our family knew just how perfectly she had nailed it: our *pushmi-pullyu* relationship balanced by a deep need to be connected, tunneled together.

That night, as I tossed my bouquet and headed for our

friend's convertible, which would take us to our hotel, I side-hugged and quickly embraced friends and family who lined the route to the car: Granny and Papa, Mom and Dad, Andy's parents, a few of my bridesmaids. And there, at the end, was Sharon. Her face was bright and smiling, glowing with sweat from leading the charge on the dance floor. She extended her arms and we held each other tight, my fingers pressing into her back, hers pressing into mine. As brides of all the ages have surely felt, this was the night of my greatest joy and the first adult experience of sadness and loss. Neither of us wanted to let go.

For Sharon and me, the road to an adult relationship has been hard, spanning decades. The conflict is more than most can tolerate, but it is an accord based on truth and honesty. As exciting new friendships crescendo and fade, as friends move away or trade up, I come back always to Sharon and she to me. We do not always like each other, but we cannot escape our love. We have worked and fought and clawed for it, have gone past the point of no return and still returned. Friends could not do this, only siblings. Because there is a given-ness in blood relation. You did not choose it, you cannot run from it, or if you do you will only run into something worse. You have to stay with it, forgive it, love it today and hate it tomorrow, forget it until it remembers you, and forgive it again.

When Sharon and I grew up and left home, I think we were afraid that separation would rob us of the intimacy upon which our violent love had always thrived. Now I think we both know we couldn't kill this thing if we tried.

No matter the miles between us, she is my center.

Pumpkin-Walnut Scones

MAKES 8

While we are different in many ways, Sharon and I are both full-blown pumpkin junkies. As soon as September first rolls around, we look for any excuse to include pumpkin wherever possible. After much testing and several iterations (and maybe a few arguments), we arrived at what we believe to be the perfect recipe. These scones are best enjoyed on a weekend morning—soft, flaky, and warm from the oven—with a cup of cinnamon-laced coffee. If you don't have demerara sugar, just sprinkle the scone tops with a little granulated sugar.

2 cups all-purpose flour

6 tablespoons sugar

2 teaspoons pumpkin pie spice

1 teaspoon baking powder

1/2 teaspoon salt

1/4 teaspoon baking soda

1 stick (8 tablespoons) frozen butter

1/2 cup pumpkin puree

1/4 cup sour cream

1 large egg, separated

1/2 cup coarsely chopped walnuts

1 tablespoon demerara sugar for sprinkling (optional)

continued on next page

Adjust oven rack to lower-middle position and heat oven to 400°F. Line a baking sheet with parchment paper or use a non-stick baking mat.

Mix flour, sugar, pumpkin pie spice, baking powder, salt, and baking soda in a medium bowl. Grate ⅓ of the butter into the flour mixture on the large holes of a box grater; toss. Repeat grating and tossing twice more. Using fingertips, work butter into flour a bit more.

Mix pumpkin puree, sour cream, and egg yolk with a fork until smooth. Using same fork, stir into dry ingredients until large dough clumps form. Use your hands to press dough against the bowl into a ball. (There may not seem like enough liquid at first, but as you press, the dough will come together. If necessary, flick a little water into bowl bottom to get the last bits to adhere.) Place on a lightly floured work surface and pat into a 7½-inch circle, about ¾-inch thick. Brush with egg white, sprinkle on nuts, pressing to adhere, and sprinkle with optional demerara sugar. Use a sharp knife to cut into 8 triangles; place on prepared baking sheet, about 1 inch apart. Bake until golden, 15 to 17 minutes. Cool for 5 minutes and serve warm, or at room temperature.

6.

The Perfect Recipe

pam

THOUGH I AM THE AUTHOR OF FIVE BOOKS WITH THE WORDS "perfect" and "recipe" in the title, I no longer believe in "perfect recipes." I understand that knowledge, experience, and practice often results in well-crafted food, but I reserve the word "perfect" to describe the connection that frequently occurs when good food is shared. I didn't always think this way.

An aspiring cook in the early 1980s, I subscribed to all the food magazines—*Bon Appetit, Gourmet, Food and Wine, Cuisine*—but I was most drawn to *Cook's* magazine. What it lacked in sophistication and glam, it made up for in seriousness and curiosity. When David was considering Yale Divinity School in New Haven, Connecticut, I couldn't believe my favorite magazine was just thirty minutes west in Bridgeport. Might there be a job opening? Back then there was only one way to find out. I wrote them a letter. I'd be moving out East in a few months. Was there a spot for me in their kitchens?

Cook's responded that they were looking for a test cook, and they'd love to meet with me. (It's a good thing I wasn't applying now. Without a culinary degree, I couldn't even get my whisk in the door.) On one of our visits to New Haven I interviewed with the food editor. It went well. I liked her, she liked me, and things looked promising. A few days after I got home, I got a letter with news that was both elating and deflating. They could offer me the job, but the starting salary was . . . drumroll . . . $14,000 a year.

Here was my dream job within my grasp, but David was just starting a three-year master of divinity program, Sharon and Maggy were just one and three, and I was the breadwinner. There was no way I could afford to take that job. Not that a few thousand more would help, but I called to inquire about wiggle room on the salary. Nada. Sadly, for now, I had to let it go.

It was a tough first year in New Haven. We had sold our beautiful home in Geneva, Illinois, and moved into a tiny two-bedroom student apartment. I had left behind a thriving catering business and returned to full-time work as a property adjustor for an insurance company. I spent my days driving around Connecticut settling Hurricane Gloria claims while exploring other food opportunities with culinary luminaries such as Jacques Pépin and Martha Stewart, both Connecticut residents at the time. Nothing was clicking, and a year in, I was miserable. David was getting his education. I needed a job that would get me on a career path, too.

Then it happened. Within nine months the woman who

had ultimately taken the test cook job got tired of her three-hour reverse commute from New York City and gave notice. I had kept in touch with the food editor, and she let me know the position was open again. I didn't know how I could afford to take this job, but I didn't care. I had been given a second chance, and I wasn't saying no.

I interviewed again. This time I had to make and style chocolate mousse *and* critique the recipe. I passed the test, gaudy whipped cream rosettes and all. They offered me the job and even bumped up the salary. I was now officially a test cook at *Cook's* magazine making a handsome $14,500 a year. Best investment I ever made.

Finally I was getting paid to do what I loved—to test and develop the recipes featured in each issue. This was 1987, and there wasn't a lot of curiosity in the kitchen yet. Harold McGee's thick tome *On Food and Cooking* had been published a few years earlier, but Shirley Corriher's *CookWise* was still almost a decade away, and Alton Brown's books didn't start hitting bookstores until 2002. Back then people had no idea why cheesccakes cracked, meringues wept, and roasted poultry breasts were dry when thighs were still pink. This kind of stuff fascinated me, and I loved the challenge of solving culinary mysteries.

Shortly after I arrived, the food editor gave notice. It was probably too soon for me to express interest, but these jobs didn't come around often, and I was ambitious. I sent out a few subtle feelers. When word reached the magazine editor, she promptly called me in and informed me that without a degree from a prestigious culinary school similar to hers and the current food editor's, I could never expect to be more than a lowly test cook. Sure enough, the new food editor she hired came from the same distinguished background.

A few months later the editorial direction at the magazine shifted, and that editor was laid off. The relative new kid on the block, I was now senior staff. Over the next three years I rose to associate food editor, and when the next food editor quit, Chris Kimball gave me the keys to the kitchen. I became the magazine's food editor.

Unlike the former editor who thought I needed to be professionally trained, Chris liked my kitchen curiosity, pluck, and tenacity. As I was testing the May 1989 article entitled "Cheesecake Classics," I observed that some of the cheesecakes were cracking and others weren't and set out to discover why. In that month's editorial Chris noted that, "Pam Anderson, our associate food editor, suggested a more scientific test—bake one cheesecake with a water bath and bake a second one without. The results were, from my perspective, unexpected." He continued, "As I read over the Cheesecake Classics manuscript later that week, I realized that this kitchen test—pitting one method against the other—is at the heart of *Cook's* editorial style." I believe this was the moment *Cook's Illustrated* was conceived, but that magazine—successor to the old *Cook's*—would not be born for a few years.

Within a year Chris sold *Cook's* to the Bonnier Group, a Scandinavian publishing company who quickly folded us after unsuccessful attempts to crack the U.S. media market. But this would not be my last encounter with *Cook's*. The following year the phone rang. It was Chris Kimball, contemplating a new magazine venture called *Cook's Illustrated*. Would I write an article for the charter issue?

We decided to start basic—with the staff of life—and I spent the better part of that winter baking loaf after loaf of bread, testing flour varieties and yeasts, different rising and baking methods, and a host of shapes. Chris liked this approach so much he asked me to write another story—sans byline—for the same issue. In my next article, entitled "Improvising Vegetable Soups," I created a simple soup formula from which I developed four seasonal variations. Looking back now, I see how those two very different stories in that charter issue—one about perfection, the other about getting it on the table—were the seeds of what would become my cooking philosophy.

In the fall of 1992, the charter issue of *Cook's Illustrated* came out, and there was enough interest to launch. The newly emerging Internet made it possible for me to work from home, and thus began my seven-year stint as a tele-commuting magazine editor. As food editor I tested all the incoming recipes, but I was also tasked with writing at least one article per issue.

From start to finish, these stories were torturous. Today, recipes are just a click away. Back then I'd start by combing my own bulging cookbook collection, photocopying all the recipes that seemed halfway relevant. Next I'd call Nach Waxman at Kitchen Arts and Letters in New York to find out what books I was missing on the subject. He'd pack up a big box and ship them out. Recipes gathered, I'd make big charts so that at a glance I could visualize the range of possibilities for each ingredient and start organizing the tests. After that, I'd make a shopping list and head to the store or mail order the hard-to-find stuff.

Then came the long days of grueling testing that started early in the morning and often extended until well after dinner. Exploring a new dish was always exciting—endless tastes of lemon meringue pie, brownies, and strawberry shortcake—but by early afternoon the first day, the fun was over. After that it was strictly work, slogging through round after round of tests, tasting when you didn't think you could stand another bite. Even some of my favorite foods like chili and ribs were hard to stomach after a full day of testing.

As tough as these recipe challenges were, there was always so much to learn, with delightful surprises at every turn. And when you nailed it, there was deep satisfaction. My ideas were shaped by the cooks who had gone before me, but I never ended up with the same recipe as anyone else. When you build a recipe from scratch, you know it intimately, and in the end you can call it your own.

This was a new way of writing about food and not everyone got it, so it was also my job to teach authors how to do the heavy research and testing that I was doing. Many loved the idea of writing for a food magazine, but given the writer's fee and what it took to write a piece for *Cook's Illustrated*, most didn't have the stamina or the stomach for it.

After seven years, I was getting tired (and fat) from the exhaustive testing. Something was shifting within me. Until now, food had been the end—a series of perfect dishes that would make (or break) my meal. Eventually I started to realize that many of the recipes I had so carefully developed in lab-like conditions often didn't work in real time. Guests run late, you get caught up in the fun, you're juggling multiple dishes, and you miss that window of perfection. When it didn't turn out perfectly, I was disappointed in myself and apologetic with my guests.

I wasn't the only one apologizing. People often confessed they were afraid to invite me for dinner because their food wouldn't be up to my standards. When I stopped to think of my own dinner parties, I knew: Most people just want to eat well and have fun. If I was nervous, so were they. If I was relaxed, they were, too. Everyone enjoyed good food, but no one cared if the meal was "perfect." Only a small minority took some pure gustatory delight in a crème brulée made one tick better with heavy cream instead of light.

We all know the kind of perfection that feels distant and haughty and judgmental, and another kind of perfection that feels welcoming, open, and affirming. I didn't really know this for sure until I ate a summer lunch in 2002.

Anne Blanchard, her husband, Monty, and their three daughters, Lydia, Catherine, and Cordelia, lived in New York City during the week, but nearly every weekend they made the two-hour drive to their home in Bucks County, Pennsylvania. At the time David was rector at Trinity Church in Solebury and attending services at our church was part of their Sunday ritual. An economics professor at Queens College, Anne was a force behind women's education and advancement. She was a couple of years older than I, and the two of us had four things in common. We were born in Alabama, we worked, we had daughters, and we loved to eat and drink well.

I first met Anne at a dinner party welcoming us—the new rector and his family—to the community. One of the first things I noticed about her was the big patch on the back of her leg, covering the wound from her recent melanoma surgery. It appeared they had gotten it all, so with some caution that night we celebrated.

Anne made it eight years before the melanoma resurfaced in her groin. Post-surgery, David and I visited her in the hospital bearing a batch of my "perfect" chocolate chip cookies. This time there were furrowed brows and no cautious celebration. Within two years the melanoma had made its way to her brain. Monty and Anne did everything they could—traditional, natural, experimental—to keep her tethered to this world.

Those last few months of her life our families shared many meals together, but the one that changed me was an impromptu post-church lunch. Those days she was eating vegetarian, and Monty had put together a bean and corn salad with some baby greens. Could we join them, and would I bring dessert? At this point in my cooking life, it was difficult for me—a serious food professional—to bring store-bought anything to someone's house. But I had nothing in reserve, and there wasn't time to make anything. It was early summer, so I picked up some local strawberries and sliced pound cake.

I don't remember what David and I were arguing about en route, but we arrived on edge to a home where we had wined and dined magnificently so many times. At this point Anne wasn't able to do much, so we all pitched in, taking mismatched plates and fast-food plastic cups out to their picnic table. There we ate like we could all die tomorrow. It was bittersweet. I don't remember anything we talked about, but David and I left that lunch moved. Something mystical, spiritual had happened around that table. Whatever we had been testy about before lunch didn't matter anymore. We were calm and in communion.

I didn't know it at the time, but this was the moment I started caring less about perfection and more about connection. I still care very deeply about serving good food, but ever since then I've come to see food more as a means to an end. For me it's a good night not when the apple tart I've made is perfect, but when the conversation has been significant, and people have made some connection of the mind or heart or spirit.

Anne died in September 2002, and I dedicated my next book to her. She is still my friend, still someone who visits me and whose love and wisdom I still know.

These days I have another friend about my age. We share many things in common, including the same first name. Not long ago Pam was diagnosed with Parkinson's, and I ache as I've watched her give up a very successful career and deal with all the physical and mental complications of the disease. One night late last summer I invited Pam and her husband for dinner with another couple I thought they would like. We dined well (the new me even allowed Mary to bring her signature pecan pie for dessert) and enjoyed one another's company. David and I were friends with both couples and wanted to get them connected, but who knew if their friendship would flourish?

A few months later Pam and I were at a Christmas party. She said, "By the way I've been meaning to thank you for introducing me to Mary. She's become such a good friend."

That dinner party with the six of us had created a new, lasting friendship. Perfect.

Classic Apple Pie

SERVES 10

Classic Apple Pie exemplifies my perfectionist style and is a result of exhaustive testing. It takes time and patience to make it, and the results are worth the effort. Baking the pie on quarry tiles is optional, but they (or a pizza stone) help the bottom crust to brown.

1 Recipe Perfect Apple Pie Filling with Cinnamon and Cognac *(page 89)*

Rich, Flaky, Easy-Roll Pie Dough

2¹/4 cups all-purpose flour

4 tablespoons sugar

1 teaspoon salt

1 stick (8 tablespoons) butter, frozen, quartered lengthwise, and cut into ¹/2-inch pieces

8 tablespoons (4 ounces) very cold cream cheese

4 tablespoons vegetable shortening, frozen and cut into ¹/2-inch pieces

¹/3 cup ice water

1 egg white for pastry wash

Prepare Perfect Apple Pie Filling with Cinnamon and Cognac; refrigerate.

continued on next page

Meanwhile, mix flour, 2 tablespoons of the sugar, and salt in a food processor fitted with the metal blade to combine. Add butter; toss to break up butter cubes and coat with flour. Pulse 12 to 14 times, one long second each. Break cream cheese and shortening into flour mixture; toss to coat. Pulse another 4 or 5 times, one long second each, until fats are pea and pebble size. Add water; pulse twice, one long second each, to evenly distribute the water. (Dough will not have come together.) Dump mixture into a bowl; press with palm of hand to form a cohesive ball.

Divide dough, making 1 portion slightly more generous than the other. Wrap each portion in plastic wrap; press each into a thick disc. Refrigerate until chilled, at least 2 hours. (Can be refrigerated 2 days or frozen 2 months.)

Adjust oven rack to lowest position; optionally, place four 9-inch quarry tiles on rack to form an 18-inch square. (A pizza stone works as well.) Preheat oven to 400°F. If using tiles, heat for at least 30 minutes.

Set larger dough disc on a floured work surface; roll into a 14-inch circle. Fold dough in half, setting pie plate next to fold line. Quickly lift dough into pie plate and unfold. Lift edge of dough with one hand and press dough into pan sides with other hand so that dough fits in pan and is not stretched in any way. Trim excess pastry dragging on the work surface; spoon in cooled filling.

Set remaining dough disc on a lightly floured work surface and roll to a 12-inch circle. Fold dough circle in half, setting filled pie shell next to fold line. Quickly lift dough onto filling and unfold. Trim dough all around to an inch beyond the pan lip. Roll overhanging dough under with fingertips so that it is flush with pan lip. Flute dough edge all around and cut vents in dough top.

Set an 18-inch square of heavy-duty foil on tiles or pizza stone. Set pie on foil and bake until dough has set and just starts to color, about 20 minutes. Remove pie from oven, brush top with egg wash, sprinkle with the remaining 2 tablespoons sugar, and continue to bake until golden brown, about 20 minutes longer. Bring foil around pie to loosely cover edges. Continue to bake until the filling bubbles, 15 to 20 minutes longer. Cool on a wire rack until barely warm, about 3 hours. Serve.

Perfect Apple Pie Filling with Cinnamon and Cognac

MAKES ENOUGH FOR 1 CLASSIC APPLE PIE OR 2 QUICK RUSTIC APPLE TARTS WITH OATMEAL CRUMBLE TOPPING

3/4 cup granulated sugar

3/4 teaspoon ground cinnamon

1/4 teaspoon salt

4 pounds crisp, firm apples, such as Granny Smith, cored, peeled, and sliced 1/4-inch thick (a heaping 12 cups)

4 tablespoons butter

2 tablespoons cornstarch

2 tablespoons brandy (optional)

1 teaspoon vanilla extract

continued on next page

Mix sugar, cinnamon, and salt; toss with apples. Heat butter in a large (11- to 12-inch), deep skillet over medium-high heat until it looks pale nutty brown. Add apple mixture; cover and cook until the apples soften and release their juices, about 7 minutes. Uncover and continue to cook until juices thicken to a light syrup, 1 to 2 minutes longer.

Meanwhile, whisk cornstarch, brandy, and vanilla in 1 cup of water; stir into apple mixture until it thickens, less than a minute. Transfer apples to a jelly roll pan to cool quickly; refrigerate or set in a cool place until apples cool to room temperature.

Quick Rustic Apple Tart with Oatmeal Crumble Topping

**MAKES TWO
9-INCH TARTS**

Quick Rustic Apple Tart with Oatmeal Crumble Topping represents my do-whatever-it-takes-to-get-together side. No time to make a crust? No problem. Just make the time to sit down and share a meal.

1 Recipe Perfect Apple Pie Filling with Cinnamon and Cognac (page 89)

2 refrigerated pie crusts from a 16.7-ounce package

Oatmeal Crumble Topping

3/4 cup all-purpose flour

1/2 cup old-fashioned oatmeal

1/2 cup dark brown sugar

1/2 teaspoon ground cinnamon

6 tablespoons butter, melted but not hot

Prepare Perfect Apple Pie Filling with Cinnamon and Cognac and refrigerate. Adjust oven rack to lower-middle position and heat oven to 400°F.

Meanwhile, mix flour, oatmeal, sugar, and cinnamon; stir in butter with a fork until well combined. Use hands to form clumps.

continued on next page

Unroll one of the refrigerated pie doughs and place it onto a
12 × 18-inch lipless parchment- or Silpat-covered cookie sheet,
so that one side of the dough overhangs the short side of the pan
by 2 inches (to make room for both complete tarts). Spoon half
the apple filling onto the dough, leaving a 2-inch border all
around. Bring pie dough over filling, pleating it to fit. Sprinkle a
portion of crumble topping over exposed filling.

Repeat process with remaining dough, filling, and crumble. Bake
until golden brown, 40 to 45 minutes. Cool slightly, serve warm.
(Can be made several hours ahead of time and warmed in a
300°F oven for 15 minutes.)

7.

Cents and Sensibility

sharon

THE SUMMER MOM WROTE A STORY ON "HOW TO COOK LOB-
ster Perfectly" was an unforgettable one. Though we
were already perennial Maine vacationers (and probably
would've gone anyway), we needed to be in Maine that summer so that Mom could get fresh lobsters fast enough and
cheap enough to test fifty different ways of cooking them.

It was the first time we rented a bona fide house in Maine,
not just a tiny cottage on stilts along the harbor. The house
was classic New England, all neat angles and clean, white
clapboard lines punctuated by smart black shutters and cozy
dormers. The large house seemed even bigger rising from
the scrubby surrounding beach trees and silhouetted against
a humbling expanse of choppy north Atlantic water. It was
drafty, even in the heat of summer, but Maggy and I didn't
mind as we each laid claim to our own bedroom—a major
step up from sleeping on daybeds in the living room. Most
important, however, this house had a *real* kitchen where

Mom could work, rather than the typical cottage galley with rainbow-hued plastic dishes, dull knives, and dinky cookware.

Despite the excitement of a big house in a gorgeous locale, there was something a bit morbid about that vacation. Mom's research was thorough, which meant she had to figure out whether the cooking method was all that mattered, or if the manner in which you killed the lobster affected the texture of the meat. Did shocking it in boiling water make the lobster's sweet, tender flesh tense into tough, stringy misery? Mom tried freezing the creatures before boiling them to disorient their little brains and relax their muscles. She tried stabbing them in the head to make the kill quick and merciful before cooking. She even tried putting them in the pot and slowly raising the heat, but the scratching inside was pretty unbearable. To prevent their tails from curling up during cooking, my dear mother rammed a stabilizing chopstick up their ass, all along the tail and into the body. Nothing produced reliable results. Mom was frustrated, and the rented kitchen was a graveyard of discarded exoskeletons whose cheery redness contrasted disturbingly with their lifeless state.

Unsurprisingly, that was the same week my sister marched determinedly up to the dinner table and announced that she wanted to be a vegetarian. Maggy said she'd been reading articles on animal cruelty and had listened to a few stories on NPR, but I think Mom's new status as a serial crustacean killer was getting to everyone. When Maggy had completed her proud and practiced announcement, Mom cried.

In another family system those tears might have been considered an overreaction, but not in ours. Maggy was rejecting an entire beloved food group—something my mom had always urged us not to do. We didn't have to like everything, she always said, but we had to keep an open mind. Maggy's fledgling conviction also threatened my mother's single most important house rule: No one gets a separate meal. How could Mom respect her daughter's wishes, while still holding a firm line that a mother was not a line cook and meals were not made to order? Negotiation ensued. Maggy agreed to eat poultry and fish, Mom signed off on the elimination of red meat from Maggy's diet, and by extension, our family's. Then, the lobster pogrom resumed.

Usually our vacations were filled with windy walks along the craggy shoreline, long bike rides in the woods, chilly mornings out on the water in rented kayaks, and evenings spent listening to the radio and playing raucous board games. That summer, however, I remember many more hours of reading and solitude. There wasn't much in the way of fun to be had unless you count eating lobster, which I do.

One afternoon, I was so bored that I shut myself in the bathroom and memorized a deck of cards. After I performed the whole pile—color, suit, number, and face—from memory, my dad decided that I could probably use some air. With a mixture of admiration and concern etched across his eyebrows, he told me to put on some shoes, get my sister, and meet him out back.

I did as I was told, rescuing Maggy from the pages of yet another book, and found Dad behind the house, hands shoved into the pockets of his ragged khaki shorts and eyes trained on the tiny outcropping of islands that grew and shrank with the tide. As was our custom, Maggy and I each took a side, slipping our hands into his to signal that we were ready to go. We picked our way along the coastline, climbing over large boulders, collecting interesting rocks and bits of sea glass, and crouching over tide pools to check for signs of life. When we got to the end of the beach, Dad stopped and sat down on a big dove-gray rock dotted with stiff yellow lichen. Maggy and I found perches on nearby stones, and we all looked out over the ocean.

At that moment, the sun came out from behind a large cloud, sending the full force of its light down onto the water and creating the kind of blinding reflection you can still see when you squeeze your eyes shut. We sat there quietly taking in the scene for a while until Maggy, of course, broke the silence: "It looks like someone sprinkled gold all over the water." Dad cracked a slightly mischievous smile, and then got up and jogged down the beach to the water's edge. When we arrived, a little breathless, at his side, he was unlacing his battered old running shoes and pulling off his socks. Maggy and I followed suit, wading after him into ankle-deep water.

Dad beckoned us to fashion cups with our palms like we were getting ready to receive Communion, and then he reached into his pocket and took out a fistful of change. Leaning ceremoniously over our cupped hands, he filled them each with coins while Maggy and I exchanged quizzical glances over his hunched shoulders.

When we each had a small handful of spare change, Dad waded deeper into the water and turned around to face us both. "I gave you this money because I want you to throw it in the water," he said, smiling. "What! Are you serious? Why?" Maggy and I exclaimed in near unison. "Because sometimes you have to be willing to sprinkle a little gold on the ocean," he continued. "You've got to throw money away—give to someone who cannot pay you back, donate to causes that will never return your investment."

He splashed back to where we were standing and turned again to face the water. "On the count of three, we're all going to throw our change. When you let it go, you have to be okay with the fact that it may never come back to you." Dad paused before going on, "This money may be found by someone who needs it more than you do, or it might find its way back to you in forms you don't expect. The point is that every now and then, you have to let money go so that it never has a hold on you."

Maggy and I just stood there nodding, not knowing what else to say but feeling the importance of the moment. On the count of three, we all flung our little pile of coins into the water and watched the shiny metal rainstorm splatter the surface and sink.

I'm not sure what made my dad choose that moment or method to drive home his point. Perhaps it was because Mom was spending so much on lobsters or because Dad felt the need to remind himself that we were really cottage people sojourning in that big house. Either way, the fact that I remember almost every detail is a testament to its efficacy.

Many times over the course of my teens, I would be reminded of that moment by the water. Mom and Dad, who refused to open their wallets and dole out twenties every time Maggy and I headed to the movies, put us each on a strict allowance. We got a set amount every month and that was it. If we blew it on pizza and clothes and couldn't afford gas, then we had to take the bus to school. If we complained about needing more cash, their answer was simple: get a job.

Our allowance wasn't just about lip balm, burgers, and fuel, though. In addition to ponying up for oil changes, car insurance, and (in my case) the actual car, Maggy and I were expected to give away a portion of our piggy bank every month. We could choose any cause, but Dad suggested we start by giving to the church. Adolescents that we were, Maggy and I chafed at his recommendation. We scarcely had any money, we argued: How could we possibly be expected to give it away? To his credit, Dad didn't argue or give examples; he just smiled and assured us that we would find a way to make it work.

Once a month, as the shiny brass offering plate made its way through our pew, I would grip my precious dollar bills and watch the approaching alms basin with about as much joy as a child anticipating a vaccination needle. The feeling of money in my hand, though, would often stir the memory of that day in Maine and the press of warm coins in my palm. "Let go," I would silently tell myself, "so that the money can't hold you."

A few years later, my dad was asked to be the speaker at my high school graduation. During his remarks he told the story of the "monkey trap." The monkey comes upon a wooden box full of bananas, and the box has a hole in the side. The monkey can reach in to grab the thing he loves, but when he tries to pull his hand out, his balled fist—now full of fruit—won't fit back through the hole. African lore had it, my father said, that once the monkey is holding the bananas, a hunter can literally walk up and grab the animal by the scruff of the neck: a monkey with such a prize in his grip would rather die than let it go. The point, of course, was not lost on all of us sitting there in cap and gown.

Though his illustration was funnier and a bit less poetic than that sun-soaked day on the beach, the effect was similar. Whatever you are holding on to that tightly—money, power, beauty, recognition—you have to let it go, or else it owns you.

When I finally started making my first salary, I was about as willing to give it away as that sullen teenager in the church pew. In his eminently gentle way, though, my dad would remind me that giving is a paradox—we tell ourselves that it will make us emptier, but its effect is nearly always the opposite. For a while, I wantonly purchased expensive shoes and downed dirty martinis with my friends without donating a dime, but I couldn't escape the whisper in my conscience (which sounded suspiciously like my father) nor the ridiculous image of that monkey stuck arm-deep in a box of bananas.

It wasn't until I was back in graduate school—living on student loans and working part-time to make ends meet—that I finally felt the urge to give stirring within me. Perhaps money had lost some of its hold on me, since I didn't have much, and now I was free to let go of some. At the time, though, I was barely making rent. The impulse to give was all well and good, I thought to myself, but how the hell was I going to make it work?

Then I met Anthony.

Anthony, who loves to cook as much as I do, rivals only my Depression-era grandmother in his ingenuity and frugality. Like Granny, Anthony will rinse and reuse ziplock bags, would die before letting a chicken carcass go to waste, and will save every rubber band, twist tie, scrap of ribbon, and packing peanut that crosses his path.

When Anthony and I started dating, we also started cooking together, and then something happened: I suddenly had money to spare. We were simmering our own stock out of scraps, making our own bread and granola, even turning spoiled milk into cheese. We started making our own salad dressing and stopped buying expensive canned beans in favor of soaking and cooking dried ones. When bread started to expire, we'd oven-dry it and make strata and bread pudding. If we needed chicken, we bought (and used) the whole bird instead of just the pricier parts.

We were saving money, sure, but we were really just having a good time. Every part of every ingredient became a challenge. We used radish greens in scrambled eggs and leafy carrot tops in frittata. We saved Parmigiano rinds to simmer in our soups and collected bacon drippings to season our pans. When a farmer at our local market was selling boxes of bruised, late-season tomatoes for pennies, we carted home twenty pounds and turned them into gallons of rich, chunky sauce. That tomato sauce became our ace in the hole. On busy nights when we just didn't feel like cooking, all we had to do was thaw a quart, cook some pasta, maybe whack up a head of lettuce, and dinner was on the table.

There were plenty of restaurants in our little city, but few that were worth revisiting. The places that turned out consistently good food were mostly out of our price range, at least for your average weeknight meal. So, we embraced the adventure of cooking at home and stocked our freezer ever higher with soups and sauces to ward off the siren call of takeout during midterm and final exams.

When Anthony and I finally moved in together, we sold my TV and bought a chest freezer with the money. With more frigid real estate and extra time on our hands without the television beckoning, we started spending free evenings and weekends on food projects. We went to a nearby orchard and picked bushels of apples for a fraction of the grocery store cost. We used them in salads, relishes, and crisps; and when they started to soften, we cooked them down into applesauce and froze it for the long, fruitless winter months. We repeated the same process when peaches came into season—peeling, slicing, and combining them with a little sugar and pectin to preserve their remarkable flavor. They, too, went into the freezer by the bagful. When we dug those peaches out in late January and spooned them—tender, sweet, and rosy—over our morning yogurt, I couldn't imagine why people ever stopped giving themselves the unimaginable gift of summer fruit in the dead of winter.

Of all the ways we scavenged and saved, the most important was probably cutting down on meat. We were never big meat eaters, but once we tried to cook without it, it seemed both easy and almost impossible. On days when we were cooking for ourselves, we could make a leafy green salad and creamy linguine carbonara with two good slices of bacon, and never pine for more prominent meat in our meals. But when hosting people, we struggled to break out of the nice cut of meat–starch–fancy vegetable mold.

Little by little, though, we began expanding our notion of special occasion meals beyond big roasts and impressive steaks. Don't misunderstand, we couldn't go full vegetarian, but meat lost pride of place at the center of our plates and found itself in supporting roles. When we started pulling off spicy chickpea korma on pillowy homemade naan, and gorgeous vegetable stews flavored with a touch of smokey pork fat and nestled on warm blue cheese polenta, then I knew we had entered a brave new world.

The first night my parents came to dinner at our new apartment, we served them earthy cheeses from the farmers' market, a voluminous salad piled high with local vegetables, and our simple, creamy carbonara made perfect by a few thick slices of bacon raised and cured a few towns away. We talked late into the evening about the troubles of the world, the ways we were working in our cities to make change, and how we were shifting our eating habits, too. When the subject of meat came up, my mom's reaction (in sharp contrast to those erstwhile tears) was one of agreement and pride. Good meat that pleases the palate *and* the planet is expensive, she said. She was glad that we were using our creativity in the kitchen to have fun and pinch pennies, and even gladder that we were finding ways to share some of that money with our community.

As they were heading out the door that night, my dad's

clear blue eyes looked a little watery as he hugged me good-bye. Maybe it was the second bottle of Syrah we opened, but I like to think it was joy that I had finally understood what he'd been trying to teach me all along. Hanging on to me a beat longer than usual, he pressed a twenty-dollar bill into my palm and then turned to leave without looking back. That worn bill felt for all the world like my investment in the ocean finding its way home.

Next day, I gave it to a homeless woman outside the grocery store.

Pasta Carbonara

SERVES 4 TO 6

This is one of our go-to recipes—it's quick and simple, and we usually have all the ingredients on hand. We love that Carbonara is light on meat, and it makes a great weeknight dinner when served with a simple green salad. You may ace this dish on the first try, or it might take a few attempts to get the hang of it. Either way, it always tastes good! The heat from the pasta cooks the eggs, but if you are nervous about undercooked eggs it's best just to skip this dish—you could coddle them, but I've never bothered to try. In all cases, I recommend using good-quality eggs that are organic and free-range.

4 slices high-quality, thick-cut bacon

3 large eggs, at room temperature

1 large onion, cut into small dice

Kosher salt and black pepper

4 large garlic cloves, minced

1/4 to 1/2 teaspoon crushed red pepper flakes, to taste

1 cup dry white wine or vermouth

1 pound long pasta, such as linguine, spaghetti, or fettuccine

1 cup freshly grated Parmigiano-Reggiano, plus more for serving

2 tablespoons chopped fresh parsley, plus more for garnish

In a Dutch oven or 12-inch skillet over medium-low heat, cook the bacon, turning occasionally, until crisp. Remove the bacon and drain it on a paper towel–lined plate. When the bacon is cool, chop it and set it aside.

Crack the eggs into a bowl, whisk thoroughly, and set aside.

Drain off all but 2 tablespoons of bacon fat, increase the heat to medium, and add the onions, a ½ teaspoon of kosher salt, and a few grinds of black pepper. Cook, stirring occasionally, until the onions are soft and translucent, 10 to 15 minutes. Add the garlic, red pepper flakes, and chopped bacon and sauté until fragrant, about a minute. Add the wine, reduce the heat to medium-low, and simmer until the wine reduces by half. Once the wine has reduced, keep the mixture warm.

Meanwhile, set a pot of salted water to boil over high heat. Cook the pasta until tender, reserving 1 cup of the cooking liquid just before draining the pasta. Drain the pasta well, dump it into the skillet or Dutch oven containing the bacon and onion mixture, add 1 teaspoon kosher salt, and stir to combine.

Remove the Dutch oven or skillet from the heat. Using a rubber spatula or wooden spoon, start stirring the pasta quickly in a circular motion. While stirring, slowly pour the eggs into the hot pasta. Keep stirring vigorously and don't stop. (If you stop or stir too slowly, the eggs will scramble instead of becoming a smooth, full-bodied sauce.)

continued on next page

Keep stirring and add the grated Parmigiano and the parsley. By now, you should have a nice smooth sauce. You can stop stirring and taste the pasta, adding more salt and pepper if necessary. If the pasta feels dry, add some of the reserved cooking liquid. If the pasta feels too wet, add a little more Parmigiano and let the pasta rest for a minute, which will give it a chance to soak up the liquid. (If you're feeling really naughty, you can add a little butter to thicken the sauce.)

If your pasta has gotten too cool by this point, you can turn the heat back on *very low* to reheat it. Serve sprinkled with chopped fresh parsley, a few grinds of pepper, and a little fresh Parmigiano.

8.

Like Parents,
Like Children

pam

MOM USED TO TELL ME THAT ONCE I GOT TO COLLEGE in the mid-1970s, her happy-go-lucky little girl got serious. When I came home on break she'd say, "You don't seem to know how to relax anymore." She was right. I was still happy, though I no longer left it to luck. And I was serious—definitely serious.

I should have said, "Mother, *you* don't know how to relax, how do you expect *me* to?" but I was too young to see family patterns, unaware that I was the only offspring of a father who didn't know how to turn his ambition into reality, and a mother who didn't know what to do with her energy and drive. I was it. This hardworking couple projected all their unfulfilled dreams onto me. I was supposed to make good.

Not long before he died, Dad finally shared the story of how he got his high school diploma. His mischievous side always ready to party, Dad had gotten himself expelled his senior year and wasn't going to graduate. Then he got lucky. His father caught the principal and a buxom teacher out in the woods, and that changed everything. His father had won him a diploma with good old-fashioned blackmail.

You could argue that a father was just trying to help his son, but I wonder if by cheating the system, Grandaddy contributed to Dad's impotent ambitions. Dad frequently said he should have been an airline pilot, could have gone to college, would have been a musician. (In his twenties Dad hung with Hank Williams, and I remember Mom buying him a harmonica to respark his musical interests.) Did not *earning* his high school diploma actually cost him his life's ambition?

Mom graduated from high school but regrets that she "didn't get much of an education." A slow reader, she wished someone had taught her phonics. But what she lacked in education, she made up for in action. For years I observed her in perpetual hummingbird-like motion, flitting from this task to that. Always moving—washing, starching, ironing, cooking, praying, shopping, defrosting, mowing, tidying, accounting, worshipping, sewing. Anything to stay busy. After her night chores she'd collapse into a recliner and promptly fall asleep. She believed "an idle mind is the devil's workshop," and she did her best to keep Lucifer at bay.

Besides being a physical dynamo, she had ambition and drive. The year I coveted the glittery banana-seat bicycle, prize for the top candy salesperson at our school fund-raiser, she helped me win it. Her strategy was two-pronged. She'd send me to pick off the little guys who'd commit to a box or two, while she went for the big kill, strong-arming business-men into buying cases of World's Finest chocolate-covered almonds. She let them know their purchase bought influence among her crowd. Though Southern women of her generation weren't taught to go into business, Mom could have racked up big numbers in sales or marketing.

By contrast, my father knew how to put in an honest day's work, but when the whistle sounded he was done. He liked a good time.

For the first twelve years of my life, Mom, Dad, and I lived in a trailer. It makes sense that our home had wheels. My father was a welder who followed the construction trade wherever work was to be found. *Ramblin'*, he called it. He and my mother moved from town to town across the South during the winter and headed up North during the warmer months. When I was five years old, they settled down in Panama City, Florida. Our lives were simple but lively. On Saturdays, after a week of working for "the man," Dad would hook up his Boston Whaler to our Impala, and we'd head out scalloping or fishing. We ended our long days in the sun with a big fry from our catch.

Mom and Dad entertained often. We had neighbors and relatives for dinner all the time, hosted church parties, and threw end-of-the-year picnics as a thank-you for all the underpaid teachers of the little Christian school I attended. Dad was the fun-loving guy who wanted to "have a big time," as he used to say. But Mom was the one who did most of the work. If we were going to have a big barbeque, she would get the house ready, shop, and prepare the food, even lay out Dad's special grilling clothes on the bed. While he babied his ribs, she would make all the sides and rush out to get him anything he needed. He sat. She scurried.

Since I sensed early on that I carried the aspirations of both my father and mother, I tried to be them both. I had the big heart of my father and the fathomless energy of my mother. I am sure I looked at my father and figured, "A big heart is not enough to succeed. I had better work my ass off." And in the world I was headed for—the professional kitchen—that would carry the day.

When I was twelve we left the trailer park and moved into a wheel-less house, one my parents bought for five thousand dollars, furnished. It needed plenty of work, and I remember my parents fixing the leaks, "antiquing" every stick of furniture, and reclaiming the yard from a riot of weeds. But only four years later they had scraped together enough to buy a piece of lakefront land. Two acres, heavily wooded, and they cleared the lot all by themselves. I could smell their ambition. I've never seen Mom more grateful than the Saturday she and Dad came home sweat-soaked and exhausted, and I surprised them with a fried chicken dinner. More than grateful, they were shocked that at sixteen I had done it all myself. It wasn't that hard. I had seen them cut up, flour, and fry chicken so many times, I knew exactly what to do.

As Mom and Dad started building their retirement home by the lake, I headed off to college, where my adult persona came out. If you could work hard and long, I could work harder and longer. College in four years? For sissies. I took heavy course loads, spent two summers in class, and graduated in three years. Three days later David and I got married and moved to Chicago, and in a very new place and in a very different way we perpetuated the work cycle.

The following year David was accepted to graduate school at the University of Chicago. When he wasn't in class he was parsing Aristotle or reading Joyce until long after midnight. Another spouse might have ended up a Dickens widow. Not me.

Eager to cook, I picked up two magazines at the grocery store checkout line one night: *Cuisine* and *Bon Appetit*. I had my Southern repertoire down cold, but those two magazines blew me out of Dixie. Here was not only a breathless array of exquisite food from the great culinary capitals of the world, but an implicit invitation to a way of life that sounded flat-out good to me: eating and drinking as the chief plea-sure and glory of life. If there was a dotted line somewhere I wanted to sign on it. *Count me in.*

Immediately I set out to cook nearly every recipe in each issue. While David spent his nights with T. S. Eliot, I en-rolled in my own kitchen counter grad school. For hours after work each night I practiced baking miniature savory and sweet tarts (I still have scores of those tiny tins), making loaf pans of bacon-wrapped country pate, and attempting puff pastry in an unair-conditioned apartment in wicked Chicago heat. Between his late-night studies and my after-hours education, we were rarely in bed before midnight.

What's a wannabe cook to do with all that food? We had parties, invited friends over for lavish dinners (following to a letter the featured menus). We hosted lavish spring buffets with grenadine-marinated butterflied leg of lamb, asparagus spears nesting in homemade puff pastry boats, and *gateau citron miroir* displayed on a mirrored plate. There were often more guests than our little second-floor apartment could hold, so our parties often spilled down the stairs, out to the porch, and onto the lawn. No one seemed to mind.

There are only so many dinners and parties a young couple on a grad school schedule and budget can afford. It was time to turn my money-sucking passion into a moneymaking business, so I started catering nights and weekends. My job was a little like my father's. He was a city building inspector who spent most of his day driving from site to site. I was a property adjustor, traveling around settling fire and water damage claims. Like Dad, I had a flexible schedule and a company car so I could get my work done and still pursue my real passion on the side. For him it was having friends over for a bowl of homemade ice cream or a rack of barbecued ribs. For me it was dropping off hundreds of decorated oak leaf cookies, which I'd stayed up all night to make, at the Morton Arboretum open house, or catering an appetizer brunch for three hundred after a Saturday morning wedding. Somewhere inside me was Dad's big heart, but I was building a business with my mother's energy.

Eventually David went to seminary and became a minister. I found my calling as a food writer and cookbook author, and together we continued in my parents' footsteps, investing big time in our girls and finding satisfaction in generous hospitality. I insisted that I would be different from my parents, but I realize now how closely we followed their housebuying pattern. We may not have lived in a trailer but, except for our short stint as homeowners in the 1980s, we mostly lived in apartments, student housing, and rectories until Sharon and Maggy were eleven and thirteen and we bought a little Cape Cod in need of serious renovation. We promptly pulled up the shag carpeting, painstakingly stripped the wallpaper, tore out saggy bathroom tile, and finally built an addition off the back. Family déjà vu.

As Sharon headed off to Williams College and Maggy headed from Kenyon to the University of Exeter in England for her junior year abroad, we bought a piece of land in Upper Bucks County before moving back to Connecticut—thick, wooded, sitting next to a little stream—and started building our dream home. Each generation thinks it is doing something wildly new as it blindly follows the only pattern it knows.

I saw it happening in my daughters. Just as I had gone into hyperdrive in college, right on cue the girls started developing their high tolerance for hard work. With Sharon it started her senior year of high school. Not willing to curb her social life and unwilling to perform at less than peak, she'd spend afternoons with friends, increasingly starting her homework as I was headed for bed, and heading for bed as I was getting up. I didn't like this new pattern, but she was good and so were her grades. I let it go. I wish I hadn't.

It got worse. In college her work/socialize binge patterns intensified. She partied all weekend, and whenever she could during the week, but when she could no longer ignore the looming deadlines she'd switch to Diet Coke and pull as many all-nighters as she could to make the grade. All I could do was sit on the sidelines and watch her self-destructive behavior. I had already said my piece; there was no telling her what to do. Like me, she'd have to figure it out herself.

Only slightly reformed now, she admits she still doesn't know how to say no. In addition to her full-time job, finishing up graduate work at Yale Divinity School, and blogging at Three Many Cooks, she's married to a minister and in the ordination process herself. She never turns down a cooking challenge. Need a wedding cake? She'll do it. Catering for a hundred and fifty? No problem. Homemade egg salad sandwiches for the homeless (with homemade bread, of course)? You got it.

Maggy can't stop herself either. Newly married and living in England, she juggled a full-time job and grad school at the University of London, all while raising thousands of dollars to fund the maternity ward that she and Andy built as an addition to a village hospital in Malawi, Africa. It's no different now. On top of an overactive New York social life, she has a big job, runs an events business on the side, and contributes regularly to our blog.

The three of us all criticize one another for not knowing when to stop. But we are all like the man in the Gospels, the one with a log stuck in his own eye trying arrogantly to remove the speck from his brother's eye. When Sharon told me that she and other church members had been asked to bake three hundred cookies and cupcakes for a gathering and that somehow, at the last minute, she was the only one left to do it, I was livid. How could she get herself suckered in? But the following week I agreed to host three church parties at the rectory. I was told a committee would be helping with hors d'oeuvres, but somehow at the last minute, I became a committee of one. Big log in my eye.

It's enlightening to connect the dots, to see how my father's impotent ambitions, my mother's unconscious drive, and their exceptional work ethic set me on course to work too hard, to see how unwittingly I passed this all along to my daughters. Enlightening, but not pleasant. I wish I could have modeled something different for my girls, but I am my mother's daughter, my father's son, really. I have taken my genes and all the bane and blessing of my culture, heritage, and upbringing and made a life. It is what it is.

I only regret to tell my mother that, despite almost never being idle, I was curiously unable to keep the devil from setting up a sizeable workshop.

Classic Buttermilk-fried Chicken

SERVES 4 TO 5

Lemon Chicken may be Dad's signature dish, but Buttermilk-Fried Chicken is my family's signature dish. It's what my parents would fry up at all those thank-you picnics for the teachers at my school. It was the dish I would surprise Mom and Dad with after a hard day of working at their lakeside property, and it is the dish my sons-in-law, Anthony and Andy, request I make nearly every time we get together. Remove the skin from the breast and thigh pieces, if you like.

> 1 whole chicken (3 to 3 1/2 pounds), cut into 10 pieces (2 wings, 2 thighs, 2 drumsticks, and 4 breast pieces, halved crosswise) neck, giblets, wing tips, and back reserved for another use
>
> 1 1/2 cups buttermilk
>
> 1 tablespoon kosher salt
>
> 1 teaspoon ground black pepper, divided
>
> 2 cups all-purpose flour
>
> 2 teaspoons fine salt (sea or table)
>
> A generous 2 cups vegetable oil (or enough to measure 1/2-inch deep in a 12-inch skillet)

Place the chicken pieces in a gallon-size ziplock bag. Mix buttermilk with 1 tablespoon of kosher salt and 1/2 teaspoon pepper. Pour over chicken; seal and refrigerate for at least 2 hours and up to 24 hours.

When ready to fry the chicken, measure the flour, fine salt, and remaining ½ teaspoon pepper into a large doubled brown paper bag; shake to combine. Working in 3 batches, drop chicken pieces into the flour mixture and shake thoroughly to completely coat. Place coated chicken pieces on a large wire rack set over a large rimmed baking sheet.

Meanwhile, measure oil to ½-inch deep in a 12-inch heavy-bottomed skillet (preferably cast-iron); bring to 350°F over medium-high heat.

Drop chicken pieces, skin side down, into hot oil; cover (with a cookie sheet or pizza pan) and cook for 5 minutes. Lift chicken pieces with tongs to make sure chicken is frying evenly; re-arrange if some pieces are browning faster than others. Cover again and continue cooking until chicken pieces are evenly browned, about 5 minutes longer. Turn chicken over with tongs and cook, uncovered, until chicken is browned all over, 8 to 10 minutes longer. While the chicken fries, wash wire rack and baking sheet and place near skillet. Remove chicken from skillet with tongs and drain on wire rack set over baking sheet. Serve warm or at room temperature. (Strain the cooled oil into a heat-safe container and refrigerate for future frying.)

9.

The Gift of Thrift

maggy

OM WAS TWENTY-FIVE AND DAD WAS TWENTY-SIX when I entered the world, and I was barely potty trained when Sharon arrived twenty-six months later. They were young parents who still had a lot of personal work to do—education to complete, careers to launch, a world to explore. When Sharon and I were old enough to start collecting our first memories, Dad was in a full-time master's program at Yale Divinity School and Mom was just beginning her dream career as a test cook at *Cook's* magazine. We lived on her meager publishing income. Years later, when Dad told me that in those days we received state coupons for free milk, cheese, and juice, I was astonished. I thought that was only for the poor, and I had never felt poor.

I was too young to remember budget details. All I know is that somehow our family lived by a simple yet important philosophy: *Whatever we have is enough.* We would live a fun, memorable life regardless of our bank balance. And thus, we lived in incredible abundance.

It was (and is) a great philosophy, but I remember the first time it was sorely tested, during Christmas 1988. That was the year my parents went to retrieve our family's Christmas decorations only to realize they had been stolen. At the time, we were living in a pint-size two-bedroom on the Yale campus. Anything not used on a daily basis, including our holiday decorations, was kept in an unlocked, unattended communal storage area in the basement.

It must have been like those first bewildered moments when you find yourself wandering around a parking garage without even registering the possibility that your car could have been stolen. Surely, it's just not where you thought you parked it! I imagine Dad being sent down to the basement to find the box, then coming up empty-handed and bringing Mom back down with him. I imagine Mom rolling her eyes as she trailed him, seeing the box in her mind's eye, knowing *exactly* where it was. They must have pushed boxes around, scratched their heads, and looked in impossible places before finally accepting that a Grinch had stolen the collection they'd been building for years. With two little girls, three and five, how would they make Christmas?

The easy option, buying new decorations, was off the table.

They told us the truth, but on the heels of the bad news— there was *great* news. We were going to make and decorate dozens of cookies to hang on the tree in lieu of ornaments. No lights? No problem! Dad was already in our cramped, galley-size kitchen popping popcorn to string alongside fresh cranberries to create a pretty garland to wrap around O Tannenbaum.

Mom set us up at the kitchen table, helped us to cut out shapes—snowmen, reindeer, and blank, bulbous baubles—and punched out a hole at the top of each, ready to string with ribbon. Each ornament was baked and decorated with glue, glitter, metallic dragees, sprinkles, and whatever else she could find. For Sharon and me, this didn't feel like a tragedy. It was Christmas come early.

For years we remembered the Christmas of 1988 and re-told the story of the stolen ornaments, recalling the mission to make new ones and the warm scent of sugar cookies in the oven and popcorn on the stove. What if no one had done us the favor of robbing us blind that year? Would we ever have discovered the gift of thrift?

Less than a year after the Christmas incident we packed up and moved forty miles south to a wealthy New York City suburb where Dad had taken a job as the associate rector of St. Luke's in Darien, Connecticut. In addition to a large church, offices, and day school, St. Luke's also had a growing outreach ministry. Person-to-Person offered a food pantry and clothing center for low-income families in the area. It was the generous response of a moneyed community, and the cast-off clothing of these people were Brooks Brothers, Lilly Pulitzer, and Chanel.

Having grown up in single-income homes, both Mom and Dad (who is one of seven children) were no strangers to hand-me-downs and weren't too proud to take help where they could get it. So as Sharon and I shot through growth spurts or when summer finally gave way to fall, Person-to-Person became our new place to shop. The clothes, mostly in perfect condition, were free.

Much like the decoration debacle of 1988, Sharon and I didn't fully comprehend that there was a problem and that Person-to-Person was a solution. Mom and Dad never made it feel like we were living some kind of subpar existence. They never justified or apologized, they just found an affordable alternative and made it fun, allowing us to root through piles of country club cast-offs to find costumes for the plays we both directed and starred in. Why shop the racks at Gap and Macy's when we could get silver heels, heavily beaded dresses, chiffon scarves, and clip-on earrings while also getting our back-to-school wardrobe?

But our joyful acceptance of this thrifty lifestyle couldn't last forever. By the time Sharon and I reached junior high, we were old enough to voice our complaints, old enough to have been influenced by a culture that valued money above all. Back when gas was a few pennies over a dollar, it was far more affordable for our family of four to drive to our vacation spots than to fly. Despite our preteen pleas, the Andersons packed up the 1991 Silver Ford Aerostar every summer, counted to three, and shouted, "We're off!" to carry on a tradition started by my dad's parents in an attempt to rally nonexistent enthusiasm at the start of a long road trip.

But what took place during those hours of prolonged confinement in a van I was ashamed to be seen in would be harder to experience on a two-hour plane ride. Yes, there was the actual vacation waiting on the other end. Yes, we remember the vacations, but the memories that have been archived into our family lore were created on the road.

We passed 22-hour road trips by listening to books on tape: Lilian Jackson Braun's The Cat Who series, Sue Grafton's alphabet mysteries solved by private investigator Kinsey Millhone, and Dick Francis's horse-racing novels. In between tapes, Mom and Dad would indulge us by planning Halloween costumes and themed birthday parties, and when we had exhausted those topics, we'd move on to writing out our inexhaustible Christmas wish lists, albeit several months in advance.

During fuel stops we'd feast on treats that were typically off-limits: Coke, corn nuts, and Bugles. When empty carbs ceased to fill the hole (meaning, we got cranky and started fighting), we pleaded for a lunch stop. Though there was a colorful parade of exit signs announcing what lay ahead—Wendy's, Subway, Sbarro, Dunkin' Donuts, Baskin-Robbins—Mom would always pull ham sandwiches, pretzels, cherries, and cookies from her box of goodies up front, the spoils of the pre-vacation fridge and pantry clean-out transformed into a lunch no Subway sandwich could touch.

As the sun set and we were paradoxically spent from sitting all day, Sharon and I would beg to go out for dinner. But we knew better. This family almost never went out for dinner. Instead, Mom would turn our hotel room into a gourmet picnic area. A big loaf of French bread, various cheeses and olives, a roast chicken ceremoniously dumped from a gallon-size ziplock bag onto a hotel tray, and a Greek pasta salad she'd thrown together from treasures of our summertime fridge—tomato, cucumber, red onion, and zippy feta.

While Mom and Dad uncorked a bottle of wine, Sharon and I ordered an in-room movie, and everyone got their reward. We'd wake up the next morning and do it all over again.

It wasn't all material for *A Prairie Home Companion.* The bonding moments were regularly punctuated by pinching, hitting, screaming, scratching, and fighting over who got to stretch out on the longer bench in the way-way back. Siblings can't help but purposefully infuriate one another, in turn provoking threats and exasperation from up front. In the last few hours of every trip, Sharon and I would inevitably crack. I'm sure Mom and Dad quietly did, too. Suffering from extreme boredom and cabin fever, we'd argue with our parents, begging them to *please* just buy plane tickets next time. We would inform them that they were welcome to continue "vacationing" like this, but we were done with road trip torture.

But these road trips became an essential story line in the narrative of our childhood. A flight would quickly deliver us from A to B, but we would have missed out on the hysteria, horror, and joy that materialized along the way. These days, the words *road trip* cannot be mentioned without recounting the now-hilarious discomfort experienced by every member of the family during Sue Grafton's requisite one-per-book love scene for Kinsey Millhone, which we all got through by pretending to be sleeping, filing our nails, or staring intensely at something out the window.

As years passed and Mom and Dad reaped the rewards of the early investment in education and entry-level jobs, the ends started to meet. By that time, though, the philosophy was ingrained—perhaps too ingrained. Mom delighted in the ability to occasionally splurge on the previously unaffordable, while Dad continued to wash the car himself, buy his suits at consignment shops, turn the heat only a tick above freezing, and badger us about turning off lights. Sometimes it caused friction, but mostly his frugality amused us.

When Sharon and I grew into young adults and moved away, we took our bags and a few boxes, but we also took those five words: *Whatever we have is enough.* Carrying this lesson with us, we were (mostly) freed from the belief that money buys happiness. We knew, from experience, that there was a richer way.

Greek Pasta Salad

Because Mom often had so many of the ingredients for Greek Pasta Salad in her pantry and fridge, she'd frequently make it for one of our many summer road trip picnics. Leaving on vacation she'd also empty out the vegetable bin and the cheese drawer and make a crudité plate and a cheese board. Add in a rotisserie chicken, some crusty bread, and seasonal fruit, and we'd have a hotel feast.

1 1/2 tablespoons salt

12 ounces bite-size pasta, your choice

2 cups seedless cucumber, medium diced and lightly sprinkled with salt

2 cups cherry tomatoes, halved and lightly sprinkled with salt

1 cup feta cheese, crumbled

1/2 cup Kalamata olives, pitted and coarsely chopped

1/2 medium red onion, sliced thin

1 1/2 teaspoons dried oregano

1/2 cup extra-virgin olive oil

3 tablespoons red wine vinegar

Ground black pepper

Bring 3 quarts of water to boil in a large pot. Add salt and pasta to the boiling water. Using back-of-the-box times as a guide, cook pasta until just tender. Drain pasta (do not rinse), pour into a shallow baking pan, and cool to room temperature. When ready to serve, place pasta, cucumber, tomatoes, feta, olives, onion, and oregano in a large bowl. Add oil; toss to coat. Add vinegar and pepper to taste; toss to coat. Adjust seasonings and serve.

10.

Mes Parents Français

pam

FALL 1988: DAVID WAS IN SEMINARY, AND I WAS CUTTING MY culinary teeth at *Cook's* magazine when one of our friends handed me a flyer, saying, "Thought this might interest you."

Our city of New Haven, Connecticut, and Avignon, France, were sister cities. Part of the relationship included a cultural exchange. The Avigonese had already been to New Haven, performing their arts and demonstrating their crafts. It was our turn to go there, and New Haven was looking for a troupe of musicians and dancers, painters and quilters, glass blowers and mimes to represent the city. It was a ten-day, all-expenses-paid journey, culminating in a side trip to Paris. To strengthen ties between cities (and save a few bucks), the group would stay with host families. They were looking for a chef too, and my friend thought of me.

David and I had spent a week in Paris the year before Maggy was born, but I had yet to explore Provence. With a husband in seminary, money was scarce, so I wouldn't be getting to France on my own anytime soon. I wasn't much of a gambler, and I didn't consider myself a chef, but the risk was low, and I had a plan.

Unlike my worthy competition, I worked at a food magazine where photographers were regulars. It was time to call in a favor. A couple of days ahead, I began to prepare all of the New England classics for my photograph—steamed lobsters, clam chowder, brown bread, baked beans, blueberry muffins, cobblers, and pies. At the end of a long day of *Cook's* photography, a colleague took the shot, which I submitted along with my application.

Like a high school senior applying for early decision, I waited. A couple of days before Christmas, the manila envelope arrived. I had been accepted. In a few months, I'd be on my way to Avignon with nineteen other artists and crafters.

On the train from Paris to Avignon, there was nervous chatter about our host families. Would they speak English? Would they take their responsibilities seriously? As someone who rarely wins anything, I was prepared to draw the short stick. As we got close to town, the group leader handed me a card with my host family's name: "Serge and Betty Beccari."

It was a chaotic arrival. Some of the families hadn't shown up yet. Others looked hospitality-challenged, but there stood Serge and Betty, an attractive middle-aged couple, smiling and eager. We quickly sized up one another's language skills. I had taken French for one year in high school and made it through college French II a decade before. In his late fifties, Serge had just started taking English. This would be interesting.

Right out of the gate, I committed my first faux pas. After putting my luggage in their car, Serge and Betty took me to an outdoor café for a little late afternoon refreshment. What did I want to drink? *"Bière, citron pressé?"* I shrugged and responded, *"Vin blanc, s'il vous plait."* White wine? They were amused. *"Non, non. Pas possible,"* they said. Wine was drunk at mealtime—*c'est tout!* This was the first of many lessons.

As part of my official duties on this trip I learned how to make do. In the absence of muffin tins for my demonstrations, I made blueberry madeleines. There were no pie plates either. Pecan tarts it would be! I also learned humility. As visiting chef, one of my responsibilities was preparing a luncheon for the sister city committee and their guests. The menu was trés American: clam chowder, followed by fried fish with coleslaw and corn on the cob. I should have listened when the chef at the culinary school where I was cooking suggested we serve the coleslaw and fish separately. In France salad always comes first, and French diners, I could tell, were polite but slightly aghast. The corn on the cob flopped, too. It was the late 1980s, when it was still a novelty in France. The chef had managed to get some from Spain, but it was animal grade. I boiled and boiled it, but it never got tender. I served it anyway, and like my mentor Julia Child, I didn't apologize for it either.

Rather quickly I realized my time in Avignon was less about the official exchange and more about my personal one with Serge and Betty. Serge adored America. There was a framed photograph of John F. Kennedy in his office, and he often repeated the story of American soldiers marching through Paris as liberators at the end of World War II. He was six years old then and would never forget it.

Lunches and dinners at Serge and Betty's were one big game of Charades meets Pictionary. In addition to plates, glasses, and cutlery, we always set the table with a French-English dictionary, maps, a big notepad, and pens. Despite the language barrier, we mostly understood one another. Eventually I discovered if I used the English word with French pronunciation, it usually worked. Celebration, humiliation, participation. *C'est la même.* But there were times when it didn't. At the end of dinner one night, to declare myself full I said, "*Je suis plein.*" They roared. I had just announced that I was pregnant.

Although I lived in Connecticut, I came to France a Southern transplant. I had learned to cook from my Alabamian mother, aunts, and grandmother. Because of them I knew how to fry chicken, long-simmer greens, and stew a roast. Simple cuisine, yes, but time-consuming for my working life. In contrast, Betty's breezy à la minute style spoke to me.

Her fridge was small, and her time was limited. She'd pick up turkey cutlets at the butcher or salmon at the fishmonger's. In a flash they were on the table with a simple sauce and seasonal vegetable. Relaxed, we'd finish up the meal with bread, a little stinky cheese, and some seasonal fruit. I liked their simple, elegant way of eating.

During those ten days I imprinted on Serge and Betty, following their every lead. I ate what they ate, drank what they drank, lived like they lived, and watched how they shopped and cooked. Before I left France that spring, the three of us had cooked up a plan for them to visit us just a few months later.

By that time David had graduated and gotten a job in Darien, and we were living in a cute little New England rectory. Sharon and Maggy were four and six, and we had two new little kittens. For Serge and Betty we were *le classic* American family. During their time with us we walked the Freedom Trail in Boston, took in a few Newport mansions, visited Mystic Seaport, and treated them to Broadway. We dished up American favorites like oyster stew and steamed lobsters and made them eat ribs and corn on the cob with their fingers. Not easy for people for whom asparagus is the only thing meant to be picked up by hand.

Now we had been there, and they had been here. We could have called it quits. After all, they had hosted me, and we had reciprocated. But our relationship ran deep. Serge had a daughter from a previous marriage. Together Serge and Betty had raised her, but their relationship was troubled. She never married, and there would be no grandchildren. And I was an only child of parents who didn't "get" me. So we all carried on. Our formal *vous* became the familiar *tu*, and for twenty-five years we were one another's surrogates—parents, children, grandchildren—taking turns visiting back and forth.

The summer Sharon and Maggy were ten and twelve Serge and Betty invited the four of us to come for a month. That's when we learned how to vacation. Earnest travelers in the past, our family would typically get up and spend hours dutifully seeing every listed site in the guidebook. By day's end we were exhausted and cranky. A couple of weeks of that, we were ready for a real vacation.

At Serge and Betty's the pace was very different. In the morning Serge would send Maggy and Sharon to the *boulangerie* to buy baguettes ... *en Français!* After *petite dejeuner*, we'd head to town to shop for lunch. Between that and the preparation, that was our morning. Lunch was a simple yet sumptuous three-course meal, always concluding with cheese. With all of the lively discussion, lunch went on for a couple of hours. After that Betty would close the shutters to block the midday sun. Drowsy from the wine, we'd all head off for a long *sieste*.

Only after the heat had subsided would we finally meander out late afternoon to a see a site like Les-Baux-de-Provence or check out little towns like Aix-en-Provence or Arles. Sometimes our outings were curious, like the time Serge tossed a couple of jerry cans in the trunk. We stopped at what appeared to be a gas station where Serge began to fill the cans with rosé from a hose and nozzle exactly like the one at our local Shell station! Appellation d'Origine Contrôlée limits the number of labeled bottles a vineyard can produce. The rest is sold generically, and we were the beneficiaries. Back at home David helped Serge funnel the wine into clean used bottles, and as we sipped rosé at dinner that night, we had fun doing the math. The same bottle of Tavel we'd pay $18 for in the United States cost Serge a mere 90 cents.

Dinners were light—often shellfish, charcuterie, or something quick on the grill ... and more cheese! Around midnight we'd kiss one another on each cheek and say "*bonne nuit.*" The ritual would start all over again the next day.

There were lots of surprises that first week. One day for lunch Serge and Betty served us steak tartar. Only afterward did we find out we had just eaten ground horse. One night we dined on grilled lamb kidneys. Another night it was big raw clams and oysters. Maggy and Sharon did their best to down them with the rest of us. Another night we went to a friend's house in Avignon for bony bouillabaisse. I was never so proud of the girls that night as I watched them navigate the booby-trapped stew. It seemed like a test, and the French were impressed that Maggy and Sharon had attempted it. From the movies, they believed American kids ate only McDonald's.

The second week Serge and Betty visited her sister in Savoire while the four of us stayed at their home and continued to enjoy Provence. The following week it was our turn to travel—to Lyon and Burgundy.

The fourth and final week Serge and Betty had arranged for the six of us to vacation in Menton, the last stop on the French Riviera before crossing into Italy. One leisurely Sunday morning, we headed into the hills to explore the little town of St. Agnes. Maybe it was the company, maybe it was a freak magical moment, but we stumbled into a little unassuming restaurant that served up one of my most memorable French meals.

Served family style, our first course was homemade hanky pasta pesto. The next course was a little tricky—

grilled lapin. Having already been tricked into eating Mr. Ed earlier that month, the kids were suspicious. If they knew it was Bugs Bunny, they'd have no part of it. Eyeing the mound of mystery meat with exaggerated legs, the girls inquired as to the species. On the spot, Serge blurted in his heavily accented English, "special French chicken." They bought it. Sharon and Maggy were well into young adulthood when we finally confessed.

In all worthwhile relationships, there are tensions, especially over extended stays where communication takes so much effort. We should have remembered the three-day fish/guest rule, but we thought our relationship was strifeproof.

We sensed mild tension one of our last few nights in Menton. David and I were in charge of dinner, and Serge mumbled in frustration at how much money we had spent. On the long car ride back to Avignon, Serge and Betty got into a tiff over the route. By the time Serge walked through his front door, he had had enough. I knew the signs. I had seen bottled frustration in my own father (and in my own self) and knew that at least for this visit, we had worn out our welcome. We were weary, too. It was our last night, and we were sick of French food and sick for home. The four of us headed into town and ate Vietnamese.

Of course our relationship survived that little blip. Eventually Serge and Betty retired to Nice, and we continued to visit them there. When Maggy was abroad in England, she and Sharon hopped a train to see them. Visiting for the first time as a young adult, Sharon was struck by how many of our family photos were displayed throughout their apartment. "I didn't realize until then how much we meant to them," observed Sharon. "It was like we were their grandchildren."

June 2012: David and I were en route from Venice, where we had vacationed with friends, to Barcelona where we were meeting Sharon and Anthony on their delayed honeymoon. Along the way we stopped in Nice for a few days to visit Serge and Betty. They were noticeably older; we were older, too. Since we had seen them last, Serge had struggled with lung cancer, but he was in remission.

The rituals were still the same. Each morning we'd have baguette and coffee on their terrace. We'd cross the boulevard for a quick dip in the Mediterranean and then head out to shop for lunch. This trip Serge mostly stayed home. Age and the treatments had weakened his stamina.

As David and I wheeled our bags into the Nice train station to leave, I was melancholy. Was it the realization that my younger daughter, married now, was only three years old when I met *mes parents Français?*

Like good parents Serge and Betty insisted they go with us to make sure we got on the right train. We boarded. They waited to leave until the train pulled away. As David and I waved good-bye we didn't know this was the last time we would see Serge.

Almost exactly a year after our visit and just one month after my father died, I got an email from Betty.

Priez pour Serge *(Pray for Serge)*

Aujourd'hui il a rejoint un autre monde celui de la seren-ité. *(Today he joined another world, that of serenity.)* Pour

moi c'est trés triste mais . . . la vie mene aussi à la mort.
(For me it is very sad, but life also leads to death.) Je vous
embrasse. (I embrace you.)

And we embrace you, Serge and Betty. You changed our
lives.

With a mother in the food business there's still no guar-
antee a child will appreciate good food. In just one month,
you transitioned Sharon from repulsion to appreciation of
barnyard-y cheeses and other curious French delicacies. She
credits you with stimulating her little ten-year-old palate.

Without your influence it's not likely Maggy would have
attempted a year's study abroad, where she eventually met
Andy. Over the centuries all those fights with the English
have created antipathy, but we know you were smitten with
her young man.

And without you, I would never have written *How to
Cook Without a Book*, which has profoundly changed the
way I cook and the way our family eats—and changed the
lives of hundreds of thousands of other budding cooks.

You did what good parents do.

Merci.

Bouillabaisse

SERVES 6

It was a proud moment for me the night young Sharon and Maggy managed to down a big bowl of bony bouillabaisse in Avignon. I can't say that I love picking fish bones out of stew either. I prefer this boneless version.

3 tablespoons olive oil, divided

2 medium onions, 1 cut into medium dice,
  the other halved and thinly sliced

1 fennel bulb, half cut into medium dice,
  remaining half thinly sliced

9 large garlic cloves, 3 left whole,
  remaining 6 minced

1 bay leaf

1/2 teaspoon peppercorns

1 cup dry white wine

1 quart fish stock (Kitchen Basics makes a good
  one) or clam broth

1 pound shrimp, peeled and shells reserved

Big pinch saffron

2 teaspoons finely grated orange zest and juice
  of 1 large orange

2 cans diced tomatoes (14.5 ounces each), drained

Salt and ground black pepper

1 pound mussels

2 pounds of white fish

3 tablespoons chopped fresh parsley leaves

continued on next page

Heat 1 tablespoon of oil in large soup kettle over medium-high heat. Add diced onions and diced fennel; sauté until tender, 4 to 5 minutes. Add whole garlic cloves, bay leaf, and peppercorns along with wine, stock, 2 cups of water, and the shrimp shells; bring to a simmer. Reduce heat to medium-low and continue to simmer, partially covered, to blend flavors, about 30 minutes. Let stand until cool and then strain. Add water if necessary to make 6 cups. (Can be covered and refrigerated a couple of days.)

Heat remaining 2 tablespoons of oil in a large soup kettle over medium-high heat. Add thinly sliced onions and fennel; sauté until tender, 4 to 5 minutes. Add minced garlic and saffron; sauté until fragrant, 30 seconds longer. Add orange zest and juice, drained tomatoes, and broth; bring to a boil. Reduce heat to medium-low and continue to simmer to blend flavors, about 10 minutes. Adjust seasonings, including salt and pepper to taste. Increase heat to medium; add mussels, then fish, lightly seasoned with salt; simmer until mussels open and fish is opaque, 4 to 5 minutes. Reduce heat to low and add shrimp and parsley; cover and let steam until shrimp are just cooked through, about 5 minutes. Ladle a portion of Bouillabaisse into each soup plate. Serve with Rouille and Golden Toast Rounds.

Rouille

MAKES ABOUT 3/4 CUP

1 small hunk baguette

1 large garlic clove

1/4 cup packed fresh parsley leaves

1/2 red pepper, roasted, peeled, seeded, and patted dry

1 egg yolk

2 teaspoons Dijon mustard

1 tablespoon lemon juice

1/8 teaspoon cayenne pepper

Salt

1/2 cup extra-virgin olive oil

Grind bread in a food processor to coarse crumbs. Measure out 1/4 cup. Reserve any leftover crumbs for another use. Return the 1/4 cup of crumbs to food processor, along with garlic and parsley; process until finely minced. Add the pepper, yolk, mustard, lemon juice, cayenne, and a generous pinch of salt. Process to puree. With machine running, very slowly add oil, droplets at a time at first and then a slow stream to continue, until you reach a thin mayonnaise consistency. Refrigerate until ready to use.

Golden Toast Rounds

**MAKES ABOUT
4 DOZEN ROUNDS**

1 long, thin baguette, sliced a generous 1/4-inch thick to make about 4 dozen rounds

Adjust oven rack to upper-middle position and heat oven to 425°F. Lay bread slices on a large wire rack. Bake until golden and crisp, 4 to 5 minutes.

11.

No More Mr. Knightley

sharon

MAYBE IT'S BECAUSE DAD WAS RAISED IN SMALL-TOWN South Dakota and Mom spent her early years in a trailer park that my parents were so keen to provide their children with an upbringing that was bigger and brighter than their own. Or perhaps they were just completely oblivious to what we actually *liked* to do. Either way, my parents were doggedly committed to the cultural edification of their children. Much to our juvenile chagrin, Mom and Dad regularly mandated our attendance at plays, museums, foreign restaurants, and the occasional film *not* starring Leonardo DiCaprio or Freddie Prinze, Jr.

They didn't actually care if we liked head cheese, raw oysters, wild mushrooms, or lamb curry. It didn't matter if we understood or appreciated what was happening during an opera or whether we could identify what, exactly, a work of art depicted. We just had to submit to the experience, preferably with minimal complaint. Mom and Dad seemed confident that fine art and good food would filter into our consciousness and wait there patiently until we were old enough to find meaning and pleasure in them.

Our parents knew that someday, Maggy and I would tire of Nancy Drew books, macaroni and cheese, and *Saved by the Bell*, and we'd want something with a little more depth and consequence. I'm sure they envisioned the quiet, triumphant moment when we would choose *The Mission* over *Mean Girls*, Sauvignon Blanc over Diet Sprite, and Bach over Black Flag or The Backstreet Boys.

That moment, however, had not yet occurred the night Mom and Dad dragged Maggy and me to the local art house movie theater for yet another Friday evening of education, which they tried to pass off as entertainment. This old movie theater was exactly the kind of place I would love *now*: a 1930s playhouse restored to its former glory. There were plush antique seats, red velvet curtains drawn over each movie screen, marble bathroom fixtures, and a tiny concession stand vending classic candies like brightly wrapped Bit-O-Honey and translucent sleeves of Necco Wafers. For an eleven-year-old girl who wanted peanut butter cups and romantic comedies, this place was a horror show.

We'd recently been at this exact theater for a showing of *The Age of Innocence*, a unique brand of torture involving dialogue I couldn't quite grasp and steamy sex scenes rendered more cringe-worthy by being viewed in the presence of my parents. None of this gave me much hope that I'd enjoy the upcoming film. That night, the glowing marquee had one word on it: *Emma*. At that point, I hadn't read Jane

Austen's novel and knew nothing of the young and relatively unknown Gwyneth Paltrow who would bring it to life.

Before the lights went down, I had already plowed through my box of Dots and begun sulking in earnest. The previews did little to inspire confidence in the coming attraction, and by the time the opening credits started I had rolled my eyes so many times it was a miracle they had not skittered onto the floor along with the black jellybeans and other so-called "candy." Within moments, however, I was captivated. The well-chosen words, meaningful glances, and delicate movements imbued the story with rich yet subtle romance and drama. And, of course, there were those dresses! Good Lord, I wanted Emma's wardrobe.

I walked out of that movie theater, my mind and body in the complete uproar, confusion, and bliss of first love—with Mr. Knightley, with Emma, with Jane Austen, with England. That week, I asked my mom to take me to the library after school, where I checked out every book Jane Austen ever wrote. Finishing those, I moved on to the Brontë sisters, Charles Dickens, George Eliot, and Elizabeth Gaskell. I was drunk on the English novel, and my parents graciously swallowed the "we told you so" and basked in the glory that The Boxcar Children and The Baby-sitter's Club had given way to the giants of English literature.

When given the opportunity to study literature at Oxford the summer after my junior year in high school, I begged my parents to let me go. The trip was expensive, but they were prepared to make the necessary sacrifices. For the first time in my life, I actually loved them for their steadfast commitment to my education. So off to England I went.

I made good friends and had a few fleeting romances, but it was the place itself that captivated me. I spent hours sprawled out on the grass of Christ Church Meadow, reading books, listening to music, smoking cigarettes, and having the closest thing to intelligent conversation I'd ever experienced with peers. I went out to dinner with my professors, attended plays, and went boating with friends. We took trips to castles, museums, and the birthplace of Shakespeare. My parents would have been bursting with pride—minus the whole nicotine thing—if I had taken the time to detail what I was actually doing. Our sporadic phone calls, which occurred in the now-obsolete venue of a phone booth, lasted barely five minutes: just long enough to let Mom and Dad know I was alive and still in possession of all my limbs, preserving minutes on the expensive calling cards that dipped dangerously into my small but precious slush fund.

It wasn't just the experiences and the people of England that I loved, it was the buildings, the streets, the air, the freedom. The first night in my room, which was outfitted with an ancient-looking fireplace and a full complement of antique furniture, I lay awake imagining the people who had read, studied, written, and slept in this very room centuries before me. As I walked home from class in the early evenings, picking my way through crowded cobblestone streets, the setting sun spilled pink light over the skyline. The sandy stones of those great buildings seemed lit from within, and the whole town glowed with an otherworldly aura. In those peachy, light-spattered afternoons, with a stack of books tucked under my arm, I didn't think it was possible to be happier.

Like a teenager desperately trying to make a warm-weather fling last beyond the first frost, I promised myself I would find a way back to England after that magical summer. For the next few years, I read and reread my favorite novels and watched every iteration of *Pride & Prejudice* produced for the big and small screen. I quietly—yet ardently—nursed a detailed fantasy of attending college there, marrying an Englishman, and living happily ever after in the lush countryside.

And then Maggy did just that.

Watching my sister live out my "dream life" as she enrolled at the University of Exeter, married a guy with a posh accent, and moved to the English countryside would have been a big and bitter pill to swallow, but for the blessed fact that my category five obsession with England was already beginning its steady downgrade to tropical storm status. Maggy and Andy were living in real, twenty-first century England, a place that has come a long way since Jane Austen first penned those famous lines: "It is a truth universally acknowledged, that a single man in possession of a good fortune, must be in want of a wife." As I visited my sister and brother-in-law across the pond, I realized that something about real England seen through my adult eyes couldn't quite live up to my carefully crafted adolescent daydreams.

I came to understand that my love of that great big isle was a slightly nerdy and hugely clichéd brand of youthful infatuation. Some girls lust after Brad Pitt; I chose Darcy, Heathcliff, and Rochester, along with the lush Lake District, the wind-combed moors, and the great houses of a bygone era. Of course, infatuation relies on an appearance of perfection. You don't want to know anything *too* real about the object of your affection, only what is beautiful, honorable, and good. But real love, as I know it, is found not only in beauty and goodness but also in quirks, flaws, and scars. As I began to uncover England's imperfections, my obsession waned.

After nearly a decade of dog-earing my eighteenth- and nineteenth-century tomes, there were new experiences I wanted to have, new perspectives and voices I wanted to hear. My bookshelves were beginning to fill with different titles: *Love in the Time of Cholera, The Bluest Eye, The Sound and the Fury, Brave New World, Midnight's Children, The Color Purple.* I watched Gwyneth's resplendent Emma after a few years and thought: "Well, this all seems a bit catty and small-minded, doesn't it?"

Finally—and most damning—I encountered England's greatest flaw: the food. Though the country, and particularly its large urban centers, is now awash in great restaurants and global cuisine, it was slim pickings during my first adventures there. With all due respect to hot and crispy fish and chips, a full English breakfast, or a warm shepherd's pie, and with apologies to my sister and brother-in-law, there is only so much excitement I can muster for meat, potatoes, and a challenging lack of indigenous produce. The first time I was in England, I blissfully and ignorantly survived on rice pudding, canned peaches, and Camel Lights. I wasn't old enough to drink, so I wasn't well-acquainted with pub menus that sounded more like a list of sexual positions or STDs than dinner options: bangers and mash, toad in a hole, bubble and squeak, spotted dick.

The more I started cooking in my twenties, the more I craved the flavors my parents had taken such pains to introduce me to all those years ago. In my kitchen, I started flirting with the heat, spice, and texture of the global south and east—southern France and Italy, Thailand and Vietnam, Greece, Turkey, North Africa, India, Mexico, and the Middle East. Most of all, though, I fell hard for Spain. Something about the unique regions and familiar-yet-foreign flavors of Spain grabbed me—smokey pimentón, briny seafood, crisp sherry, spicy chorizo, grassy olive oil, earthy cheeses, tender mushrooms, juicy oranges, rich chocolate, and racy, complex wines.

The first year we were together, Anthony and I both started crushing on the Iberian Peninsula while watching José Andrés's PBS cooking show *Made in Spain*. Each episode would transport us to a new region of Spain, introducing the indigenous ingredients, distinctive dishes, and local culture of that place. Once José had finished fishing for octopus, picking citrus, pressing olives, sampling wine, or learning about cheese-making, he would shuffle us back to his home in the States and integrate the region's distinct ingredients and flavors into recipes for the home cook.

Armed with José's books and encouraged by his effusive descriptions—"this is an *astonishing* tapa!"—Anthony and I set about cooking our way through Spain. Garlicky mussels from Galicia, paella from Valencia, *pintxos* from Basque country, white gazpacho from Andalucia, *arroz con leche* from Asturias.

The first time I knew I was truly, madly, and deeply in love with Spain was the first night we made Galician empanada de pollo, a huge turnover stuffed with roast chicken, sautéed bell peppers, and caramelized onions, and seasoned liberally with garlic and pimentón. On the pages of the cookbook, the empanada was impossibly gorgeous, all shiny and golden brown. The recipe seemed straightforward enough, but I knew there was no way we could pull off something so pretty and perfect. Anthony and I pressed on, knowing that even if it turned out to be a mess, it would be a tasty mess.

After roasting and pulling the chicken, cooking down all the vegetables, making the dough, shaping and stuffing the empanada, and finally, baking the damn thing, we were decidedly *less* optimistic about how we'd feel if it didn't turn out well. But when we pulled our empanada out of the oven, I just about fell over. It was even more stunning than the photograph, and it smelled like rich, toasty, meaty, smokey heaven. Anthony and I could barely wait until it was cool enough to handle before cutting enormous pieces and devouring them with crude, open-mouthed bites that let the heat escape as we chewed. It was, true to José's word, *astonishing*.

You need only one guess to figure where Anthony and I spent our honeymoon. With the help of family and friends, who contributed to our honeymoon fund rather than buying us wedding gifts, we planned the trip of a lifetime: a month traveling around Spain, seeing and tasting the places we had come to love in our tiny Connecticut kitchen.

Though we married in December, Anthony and I decided to wait until summer to embark on our big adventure. A few days after graduating from seminary, we packed up our apartment, said good-bye to our friends, and shipped all our belongings to Atlanta, which would later become our home. The sweat from hauling boxes in sweltering heat was barely dry as we boarded the plane to Madrid. To this day, I could list every single thing we ate and drank on that trip. Suffice it to say, the fact that we could still button our jeans by the end of the month was a miracle, or maybe our waist-lines were saved only by our lugging heavy hiking backpacks across the better part of the peninsula.

True love, as I said, can never be about perfection. And though our affair with Spain has certainly had its moments of sheer glory, we've also been through the mundane. A random sampling: the day Anthony got food poisoning, the tasty but awkward meal we shared in a bar that didn't take kindly to tourists, the time I watched our innkeeper physi-cally throw a kitten (yes, a *kitten*) out of her house, or the afternoon we got lost during rush hour without a map in a manual transmission rental car in downtown Oviedo. I don't quite know how to classify the night Spain won the Eurocup and we got two eyefuls of a very naked man celebrating in the middle of a traffic circle holding a burning red flare.

But the most troubling memory I have from our trip is not about Spain's flaws, but my own.

It was late into our honeymoon, and we were spending a few days in Asturias—a region famous for sweeping views of mountains plunging straight into the sea, astringent hard cider, rich beef from cows grazed on steep hillsides, seafood pulled fresh from the ocean, and pungent Cabrales blue cheese.

Anthony and I were on a cider and cheese tour in a tiny

village with a small group of Spaniards. It was cloudy in that close, misty way you only encounter in the mountains, and we spent hours traipsing across muddy fields, through gnarled orchards, and deep into musty caves. Anthony tried valiantly to translate the regional dialect and farm-specific vocabulary into English for my benefit, while I mostly nodded and smiled. Somehow the process of turning apples into hard cider and milk into blue cheese really does transcend language barriers (with the help of some wild gesticulation), because I was mostly able to grasp the intricate processes.

The tour ended with a tasting meant to showcase the region's culinary treasures. It began with thin, crispy corn cakes that we were invited to smear generously with Cabrales blue cheese and drizzle with honey. I had already consumed an embarrassing number of these and drunk my fill of cider when I realized the "tasting" was actually going to be a seated six-course meal.

I happily sampled creamy bean soups and regional sausages, but by the time we got to *papas fritas* (French fries) smothered in local blue cheese sauce, I was *seriously* struggling. I smiled weakly and nibbled at each passing course— saying "no, thanks" was clearly not an option. By the end of the meal, my breaths were coming quick and shallow, sweat was beading quietly at my hairline, and the waistband of my jeans felt like a vise grip.

In an effort to get some relief, I slipped outside for air after yelping a panicked "No!" when Anthony asked if I wanted to buy any of their products to take with us. I wound up leaning against a nearby building trying to catch my breath, willing my stomach to hang on tight and cursing myself for getting in this position. The tiny Spanish ladies around me had packed in *way* more food, and yet they were happily puffing their postprandial cigarettes a couple hundred feet away.

When I realized that the building I was leaning on was a pig barn, I actually thought: "Well, I guess if I need to lose my lunch . . . this isn't the worst place to do it."

A slow stroll through the village, some deep breaths, and I managed to hold on to my meal, if not my dignity. As I wandered through the tiny town in utter misery, I silently scolded myself for taking it too far. I loved the food of Spain so much that I'd made myself sick on it.

Looking down at my taut, distended tummy, I recalled Mario Batali and Gwyneth Paltrow's cookbook *Spain . . . A Culinary Road Trip*, which someone had given us as a gift. The big, glossy book is full of photographs so perfectly staged that they verge on satire—happy, wealthy people cruising around a gorgeous European country in a convertible, hair perfectly windswept, expensive clothes hanging just so, heads tilted back in exaggerated mirth. And, of course, Gwyneth never looks full, much less stuffed to the point of ralphing near the livestock pens.

The full-circle irony of the moment did not escape me. Here I was having my first "fight" with a country I'd genuinely fallen in love with, haunted by the image of perfection that had first inspired my powerful, but short-lived, obsession with England. "Fucking Gwyneth Paltrow," I muttered to myself as I made my way back to the car.

The truth of the matter is that Anthony and I fell in love

with Spain and with each other over our stove, oven, and table, and then we fell all over again while touring that country together. Even strung out on blue cheese and cider and feeling like a bit of an idiot, I knew that this great, real love was better than all the empire-waisted dresses I could ever wear, all the luxurious balls I could never attend, and all the subtle glances I could ever want from a slightly over-starched Mr. Knightley.

Empanada de Atún

(GALICIAN-STYLE TUNA EMPANADA)

**SERVES 6 TO 8 AS A LIGHT MAIN COURSE,
MORE AS AN APPETIZER**

Though we adore the chicken empanada described in this story, it is a serious labor of love. Making it with good-quality canned tuna saves a lot of time, but it's still more of a weekend venture than a weeknight dinner. Since Galicia is a region known for its incredible seafood, using tuna in place of chicken is both delicious and appropriate. This recipe is based on José Andrés's *astonishing* empanada, but we have changed it over the years as we continue to make this for the people we love.

For the filling:

Extra-virgin olive oil

1 pound mushrooms, such as cremini or shiitake, sliced

Kosher salt

Black pepper

2 large Spanish onions, halved and thinly sliced

2 red bell peppers, seeded and thinly sliced

2 green bell peppers, seeded and thinly sliced

4 large garlic cloves, minced

1 teaspoon sugar

1/2 teaspoon dried thyme leaves

2 bay leaves

continued on next page

1 cup dry white wine

10 plum tomatoes (fresh or canned),
cut into small dice

1 tablespoon sweet pimentón (smoked paprika)

4 cans (5 oz. each) of tuna, preferably solid
white albacore

For the dough:

1 1/2 teaspoons dry active yeast

1/2 teaspoon sugar

3 cups all-purpose flour, more for dusting

1 1/2 teaspoons table salt

1/2 teaspoon pimentón

1 large egg, beaten

MAKE THE FILLING: Heat 1 tablespoon of olive oil in a Dutch oven or large saucepan over medium-high heat. Add the mushrooms, working in batches if necessary. Season to taste with salt and pepper, and sauté until nicely browned. Remove mushrooms from the pot and set aside. Reduce the heat to medium-low and add 3 tablespoons of olive oil to the pot. Add the onions, peppers, garlic, sugar, 2 teaspoons of kosher salt, and a few grinds of pepper, and cook, stirring occasionally, until the vegetables are very tender, about 40 minutes. Add the bay leaves and thyme and continue to cook until the mixture turns golden, another 10 minutes. Add the wine, increase the heat to medium, and cook until it evaporates. Stir in the tomatoes and pimentón and cook until almost all the liquid evaporates, 10 to 15 minutes. Add the tuna and mushrooms, cook for another 5 minutes. Remove from heat, discard the bay leaves, and season again with salt and pepper, if necessary. Transfer the tuna mixture to a colander or fine-mesh strainer set over a bowl, and let cool. Reserve the liquid that strains off for making the dough.

MAKE THE DOUGH: Dissolve the yeast and sugar in ¼ cup of warm water. In a food processor fitted with the dough blade, combine the flour, salt, and pimentón. With the motor running, add the yeast mixture and ¾ cup of the reserved liquid strained from the filling. If necessary, add more filling liquid (or water), 1 tablespoon at a time, until the dough comes together into a slightly sticky ball. Transfer to an oiled bowl, cover with a damp kitchen towel, and allow to rise for about 1 hour.

ASSEMBLE AND BAKE THE EMPANADA: Heat the oven to 400°F. When ready to bake, turn the dough out onto a lightly floured work surface and cut the dough ball into 2 equal halves. Using a rolling pin, roll the first piece of dough into a 12 × 18-inch rectangle. Brush the back of a large rimmed baking sheet with some olive oil. Transfer the first rectangle of dough to the back of the baking sheet. Spoon the filling all over the dough, leaving a 1-inch edge. Brush the edge with the beaten egg. Roll the second piece of dough to a 12 × 18-inch rectangle and place it over the filling. Fold the dough edges together, crimping them with your fingers to seal. Brush the top of the empanada with the egg wash, sprinkle with a litte more pimentón, and prick the top with a fork to allow steam to escape. Bake until golden brown, 25 to 30 minutes. Remove from the oven and transfer to a wire rack to cool. Serve warm or at room temperature.

17.

Refrigerator Resurrection

pam

WAS RAISED BY TWO DEPRESSION-ERA BABIES. MOM WAS THE youngest of thirteen children, only ten of whom survived. She tells the story of their moving every time the rent came due and recalls a dozen eggs feeding ten kids and two parents. As though it were yesterday, she wistfully recounts the year she got skates and a toothbrush holder for Christmas. She was giddy until her brother wrecked his skates, and both pairs were returned. That same day her sister broke her toothbrush holder. All of Mom's many lean Christmases blend together, but she can't seem to shake that one childhood holiday of such bounty and loss.

Mom was a city girl—Montgomery was her town. Dad and his brother grew up on a small farm in La Pine, about thirty miles south. Money was scarce, but his mom and dad owned a little white house with a tin roof and an outhouse out back, and they lived off the land. It still makes Mom crazy that her family had to eat watermelon down to the white while Dad's family ate the heart and threw the rest to the hogs. Still, his family was cash poor. For Dad, Christmas was an orange and a couple of peppermint sticks.

Both of my parents were scarred by that 1930s culture of deprivation, so it's understandable they would be relentlessly conservative—religiously, politically, and socially. Financially, too. Mom was a coupon clipper, and neither would buy anything unless it was at least fifty percent off.

The older they grew the slower they were to part with things. Mom may have been fastidiously clean—every surface in her house gleamed—but open a drawer and it was brimming with the random stuff they had collected for the thirty-six years they lived in their final house. A few months before Mom and Dad moved into the retirement home, I finally talked them into letting me burn thirty years of bank statements, but Dad stubbornly refused to let me toss a telephone receiver and dangling cord I found stuffed in a dresser drawer. "I might need that someday," he insisted.

I was born in the optimistic, procreative postwar era. I did not get the conservative gene. I enjoy spending money, and when it comes to religion and politics I swing left. My guiding principle: If you don't need it, toss it. My liberal nature is pretty consistent, except when it comes to food. In that department I'm my mother's daughter. She didn't waste food, and I can't bear to either. While some people seek out perfect fruits and vegetables, she and I take pride in giving the bruised, flawed, and over-the-hill a second, glorious life.

I'm not exactly sure when I started following in her footsteps, but the turning point might have been the early 1980s when I was catering and Mom offered to help with one of my jobs. I gave her the very simple task of peeling and seeding tomatoes for a Julia Child recipe. She complained the whole time she worked on those tomatoes. Not that she minded the work. (I'd seen her shell field peas and pecans until her thumbnails almost came off.) She just couldn't understand why the tomato seeds and all that accompanying good juice needed to be extracted. To her it seemed wasteful. To make matters worse, I took the large bowl of tomato seeds and juice and flippantly flushed it down the toilet.

She has yet to let me, or Julia Child, live that down. Almost as frequently as she recounts the story of that present-less Christmas, she loves to rail on Julia's silly tomato technique and rag on me for such wasteful behavior.

I may have rolled my eyes at the time, but eventually I came around. At some point I started to see food as sacred and the act of mindlessly wasting it as sinful. I'm not frugal like Mom—I spend lavishly on food and spirits—but we share a reverence for food and the belief that it should nourish and satisfy until it's gone or gone off.

I remember my frugal foodie side manifesting itself on early family vacations. We'd rent a place in Maine or Nova Scotia for a couple of weeks. Some people might load up the car with sports equipment, games, or extra clothes for going out. Not us. Half the trunk was taken up with food from our home fridge, freezer, and pantry and wine from our cellar. Why pay twenty bucks for a small bottle of olive oil in some country store when I had a perfectly good (and cheaper) bottle I could bring from home? The same was true for my hunk of parm, the jar of capers, the can of nuts, the last few slices of smoked salmon, and my good wine. I'd pack it all up, and for the first several days of vacation we had our own little commissary. Except for the occasional round of miniature golf, box of saltwater taffy, and a few purchases at the local bookstore, our family contributed very little to the local tourist economy. We always took pride and also felt a little bad about that.

Maggy and Sharon have followed in the BYOF tradition. In fact, Sharon's husband, Anthony, is even more hard-core than I. When they first started dating, Sharon recounted how he'd made a pot of soup from "kale that was about to go bad," and at a recent dinner party he had asked for the chicken carcass the host was about to toss. Now, that's my kind of gutsy. I knew he was the one.

Sharon and Anthony always travel with food, and when they visit we provide a bedroom for the lovely couple, fridge space for their food, a freezer shelf for recharging the ice packs, and a parking spot for their cooler. Given my bulging fridge, cramming in food can be like finding bed space at a slumber party. It's tight, but you find a way.

We're often beneficiaries of their culinary booty. It might be blood sausage they picked up at a Spanish market, fresh eggs from a farm they passed, or doughy beets begging to be put out of their misery. When Sharon and Anthony are ready to leave, they pull the icepacks, pack up, and move on to the next place. To some, traveling with your own food supply may sound loopy. For us this is perfectly normal culinary etiquette.

Maggy and Andy live in New York, a town where eating out is the norm and eating in means dialing out. But now with a CSA (Community Supported Agriculture) and eating mostly vegetarian, they've taken to packing their staples. Unlike most New Yorkers who pick up a picnic before a concert in the park, Maggy makes theirs. They frequently get out of town for the weekend, and she's proud of the picnics and snacks she packs for the car. They also know where to bring their produce in crisis. I can revive deteriorating baby lettuce, give last week's dimpled corn a raison d'etre, or find a home for a lonely zucchini.

My frugal foodie side also means I won't part with food until I'm sure it's totally gone. Someone finds a suspicious-looking container of red sauce in the fridge and holds it out tentatively for me to smell—surely it's gone bad. I jam my finger in the stuff, taste it, and pronounce it just fine. My family jokes, in fact, that the epitaph chiseled on my gravestone will read, "S'fine."

My pantry-tentativeness has earned me the nickname Mary Poppins. Like the magical nanny who could pull from her bottomless carpetbag whatever the children needed—medicine, coat racks, magical umbrellas—I can pull anything from my pantry. Looking for coconut? From my very modest pantry I can offer up coconut water, coconut juice, coconut drink, coconut milk (regular and light), and coconut oil. But that's not all. I've also got sweetened flaked coconut, unsweetened coconut, coconut flakes, and a product called dried young coconut. This is just one ingredient, and the list goes on. My condiment collection has gotten so large that David (unhappily) leases out half his garage beer fridge to me.

Now that I live in two places, my culinary savior complex has gotten even more complex. After Hurricane Sandy, I vividly remember salvaging two refrigerators and a freezer full of food at the rectory in Connecticut. We hosted candle-light dinners for days only to drive to our powerless home in Pennsylvania where I triaged another freezer and refrigerator full of perishing perishables.

Even in normal times we're back and forth between houses. As the beneficiary of all my culinary salvation, David doesn't say much about the overstuffed, oversized bags of food I haul between places. It's a little kooky, but I never know when and with what I might be able to pull off a save.

Not only have I passed on my BYOF behavior to Maggy and Sharon, I have apparently given them the savior complex, too. Just the other day, Maggy texted Sharon and a few of my friends. "I just pulled a Pam Anderson. Soliciting guesses for what I did." My best friend immediately responds, "Pulled something moldy out of the fridge and said, 'Oh, that's fine.'" "DING, DING, DING," Maggy texts. "Terrie takes it!"

The very next day Sharon posts on Facebook, "Took every old/weird cheese in the fridge and made the very best mac and cheese. Who knew blue, Brie, pepper jack, mozzarella, old cheddar, Camembert, and random other crap would make a great combo?"

For me Sharon's Cheese Drawer Mac and Cheese should be the most satisfying moment for a cook. It's easy to whip up something impressive with pristine ingredients at your fingertips. But when you've got the chutzpah to take something most would toss and then transform it into a culinary masterpiece, that's when you know you're good.

Cheese Drawer Mac and Cheese

SERVES 8 TO 10

We've made this mac and cheese scores of times and never found a cheese combination that didn't work.

For the mac and cheese:

6 tablespoons unsalted butter

1/2 medium onion, finely diced

6 tablespoons all-purpose flour

1 heaping teaspoon Dijon mustard

1 quart whole milk

1/2 teaspoon dried thyme leaves

1 bay leaf

Salt

1 to 1 1/4 pounds grated cheese—anything!

3/4 teaspoon Worcestershire sauce

3/4 teaspoon Sriracha or other hot sauce

Freshly ground black pepper

1 pound small shells

For the bread crumb topping:

1 1/2 cups fresh bread crumbs

1/4 cup grated Parmigiano-Reggiano

2 tablespoons chopped fresh parsley

1 1/2 tablespoons olive oil

Salt and ground black pepper

continued on next page

Heat the oven to 400°F and put a large pot of well-salted water on to boil.

In a Dutch oven set over medium heat, melt the butter. Add the onion and cook, stirring occasionally with a wooden spoon, until very soft. Add the flour and cook, stirring, until slightly darker, 1 to 2 minutes. Stir in the mustard.

Switch to a whisk and gradually add the milk, whisking constantly. Go slowly at first, whisking until the mixture is smooth before adding more milk. When all the milk is in, switch back to the spoon and stir in the thyme, bay leaf, and ½ teaspoon salt. Let come to a bare simmer, and cook, stirring frequently, for 15 minutes to meld the flavors. (When you dip your wooden spoon in the sauce and run your finger through it, it should hold the line clearly.)

Discard the bay leaf. Add the cheese, stirring until melted, and then add the Worcestershire and Sriracha. Season to taste with salt and pepper. Keep warm, stirring occasionally.

Cook the pasta in the boiling water until (very!) al dente. Pour into a colander and drain really well. Add the pasta to the cheese sauce, and stir until well combined. Generously season to taste with salt and pepper. Spray a 9 × 13-inch baking dish with nonstick cooking spray and spread the pasta in the dish.

In a small bowl, toss the bread crumbs, Parmigiano, parsley, olive oil, and a light sprinkling of salt and pepper. Scatter the crumbs evenly over the pasta. Bake until the crumb topping is golden, about 15 minutes. Let rest for 5 to 10 minutes before serving.

13.

Eating Is Believing

sharon

'VE ALWAYS BEEN SOMETHING OF AN EMBARRASSED CHRISTIAN. Though Dad is a minister, and Maggy and I *literally* grew up in the church, I have never been particularly forthcoming about my faith.

I remember being at a wedding with my grandparents when I was a kid. A traditional Baptist affair in the Deep South, the reception was held in a church hall decked with crepe paper and balloons. The only beverage on offer was a brightly colored punch foamy with melting neon sherbet, and there was no music or dancing to be had. Maggy and I were bored, absentmindedly nibbling on tea sandwiches, cracking our teeth on Jordan almonds, and counting the seconds until we could shuck our special occasion clothes in favor of shorts and T-shirts.

My grandparents, however, were in their element, surrounded by folks who attended their church, lived on their street, and moved in their circles. At one point, Granny and

Papa sat down at a table with one of the few couples they didn't know, and asked point-blank, "Have you asked Jesus Christ to be your personal Lord and Savior?" No greeting. No attempt at small talk. Just *BAM!* I couldn't tell you what the strangers said in return. Maybe they answered with a resounding "Yes!" and the conversation continued, or perhaps they mumbled something and wandered away. The only thing I recall is how I felt: mortified.

A few months later, Granny and Papa came to visit us in Pennsylvania. As was their custom, they walked to my school around lunchtime so we could share a meal. I was already unpacking my lunchbox as they folded their adult-size bodies into child-size chairs. Just as I was biting into my pepperoni and butter sandwich, Papa stopped me: "Sharon, we need to pray first." I was in third grade. I should have been oblivious to what other kids thought, but I wasn't. I already knew that religion wasn't something you did in public, that school lunch wasn't a meal normal people prayed over. Flushed deep red with shame, I accepted their outstretched hands and bowed my head as my grandfather uttered a few reverent words over my chocolate milk, white bread sandwich, and carrot sticks.

At the time, my embarrassment was confusing to me. I didn't mind going to church on Sundays (though it wasn't like I had a choice). I found my dad's sermons engaging, and I loved the familiar hymn tunes and the alternating rumble and chime of the organ. On my best days, I was sort of awed by the whole idea of Communion and I recited the Lord's Prayer with gusto, trying to really *mean* those words I'd said a million times: "Give us this day our daily bread, and forgive us our trespasses as we forgive those who trespass against us."

I enjoyed baking cookies with the older ladies, helping out with the Christmas pageant, sharing meals with folks living with HIV/AIDS, and sitting in the silent, darkened sanctuary on Good Friday. I looked forward to Wednesday nights when the youth group would gather, and though the allure of cute boys was sometimes stronger than that of the Almighty, I remember the songs we sang, the prayers we offered, the service we did in the community. Most of all, I remember how I felt: safe, loved.

If I adored our church community so much, then why didn't I want to shout it from the rooftops? What was *wrong* with me?

I remember the first time I heard the passage from Matthew's gospel that urges those who pray *not* to do it on street corners where all can see, but in the privacy of their rooms. Folks praying in public who are admired for their piety have already "received their reward," the gospel writer says. "Yes," I thought to myself, "that's it! I'm no show-off. Praying in secret is what I am supposed to be doing!" Somewhere deep in my gut, though, I knew that wasn't the whole story.

A voracious reader and lover of literature, I was fascinated by the stories in the Bible—floods and rainbows, coats of many colors, talking donkeys, people-swallowing whales, chariots of fire, and, of course, a humble baby-God born in a stable. Certainly the Bible had some helpful lessons for my life, but so did Lucy Maud Montgomery's Anne Shirley, and Jane Austen's Elizabeth Bennett, and Robert Graves's Emperor Claudius.

I didn't particularly love the Bible more than I loved other books. In fact, the Good Book was more confusing and troubling than other, apparently less "good" ones. The Bible used words I didn't really understand and contradicted itself more often than I thought it should. How could I be instructed to pray in secret and yet be told to "Go forth and make disciples of all nations?" To say nothing of the fact that parts of the Bible weren't terribly well written. If God was the supposed "author" of this text, then I was slightly disappointed that Kurt Vonnegut, Maya Angelou, Salman Rushdie, and Louisa May Alcott were a lot better at writing than the Holy Spirit.

As I moved through my teens, my self-consciousness about faith continued. Although, to be fair, at sixteen what *wasn't* I self-conscious about? I remember seeing commercials for praise music CDs, and cringing as the camera panned over thousands of blissed-out Christians singing with their eyes closed and their hands raised. "That is *so* not me," I thought. These infomercial Christians looked so vulnerable and yet so sure of themselves at the same time. I wasn't sure about *anything*, especially not how (or if) God was at work in my life. But surely, I thought, there had to be another way to be faithful that *didn't* involve singing bad Christian rock with my eyes closed.

Mom and Dad liked the idea of religious education, but Episcopal schools were rare and pricey. So Maggy and I did six years each in an all-girls Catholic school, and with that, religion and faith really were everywhere. We ate breakfast together as a family every morning, and Dad would try to sneak in a prayer over our toast if we weren't too busy finishing homework, looking for stray kneesocks, or fighting. When we arrived at school, we were greeted by nuns and morning announcements that opened with prayer. We prayed before soccer games and school plays. When we got home, our family prayed over dinner. During the meal, we'd inevitably wind up talking about church— the people, the music for Sunday, how the new building was coming. In the evenings, I would wander by Dad's upstairs office and I could hear his voice muffled behind the closed door, practicing his sermon for Sunday.

Religion was, indeed, everywhere. A thread so thoroughly woven into the fabric of my life that it had no pattern of its own. It was the water I was swimming in, the air I was breathing, and as such, it didn't feel like it really belonged to me. It didn't feel like a choice. I hadn't asked Jesus to be my own personal anything. I wasn't sure I wanted to.

When I got to college, I was no longer surrounded by family or by that warm, faithful community that knew and loved me. There was no prayer before classes or sports games. There were no home-cooked meals blessed by familiar words. When it was my decision whether to hit snooze on Sunday morning or get up and go to church, I'll give you one guess where I spent my Sabbath.

That comforting, ever-present blanket knit of community, love, and faith had been ripped off me faster than I could kick my parents out of my dorm during freshman orientation. I struggled and floundered—lost myself, found myself, and then lost myself again. The time had come for me to choose a faith of my own, and I was adrift.

Part of the problem was that religion was just my regular

old life. I had grown up in a house where church wasn't particularly mystical because it was Dad's job. It would be like trying to feel reverence for a bank if my dad were the branch manager. And it wasn't just my dad's job—it was *all* of our jobs. Our whole family was a part of the cast, each of us with specific roles to play. We had to make "church" happen for other people on Sundays, during Advent and Lent, on Christmas Eve, Christmas Day, and Easter morning. We were the stage crew that never really got to enjoy the show.

Perhaps it was precisely because I'd stood backstage and watched the show so many times that the older I got the less that kind of worship had the power to move me. The choreographed rituals and elaborate costumes didn't appeal. The beautifully composed prayers sounded hollow to my ears and the thin communion wafers felt insignificant on my tongue. Religion that didn't touch the ground—that didn't get dirt under its fingernails—was of no use to me.

When I eventually went looking for God on my own, what I found was so desperately and blessedly ordinary. Although I'd been raised in a family that experienced as work what other people felt was holy, I finally realized that our parents were masters at creating sacred space *everywhere* since church would never be for us, the actors and stage crew, what it was for the audience. We made (and continue to make) rituals out of normal life—out of long walks, cocktails in the kitchen, moments in the car, lazy breakfasts on the porch. Dad will whip out his Book of Common Prayer to bless my new apartment, my sister on her birthday, or my husband on the day of his ordination. But he will just as easily pull out his phone while we're gathered in the kitchen to read us the poem of the day, spilling quiet blessing into our coffee along with milk.

It was, no doubt, my father who taught me how to pray, to read the Bible, and how to sanctify ordinary time. I carry with me his profound reverence for words and his deep, quiet love of God. But it was my mom's gritty, bone-deep faith that finally saved me. Though my mother is a profoundly spiritual woman, she's more comfortable leaning over the stove than kneeling at an altar. Mom lives out her love of God through love of people, and she shows that human love best in the kitchen.

My mother has always been the reinforced steel backbone of our family, and, by extension, our community. She cooked for old people and new parents, lonely folks and busy meetings. She cooked for sick patients and grief-stricken families, the rich and the poor, the friendly and the not-so-friendly. Most of all, she cooked for our family. Mom made sure breakfast was on the table every morning and dinner every night. She packed lunches worthy of James Beard Awards (whether we wanted them or not) and always had interesting snacks waiting when we arrived home. Mom provided us with sustenance, stability, the structure of good food, and the right times to enjoy it, and she taught us the beauty and importance of sharing meals with others.

Both my parents are sharp, but whereas my Dad is bookish and introspective, Mom has always excelled in street smarts and intuition. She'll swear up and down that she's not great with crowds, but can charm a room with a handful of laughs, a few off-color jokes, and a big smile. Though Mom will often attempt to bow out of theological conversations or cry uncle if Dad and I try to drag her into one of our discussions of the Bible, she *lives* it better than most people I know.

Hers is not a conditional love. It feels divine in its very depth and potency. Showing up in the kitchen to talk with Mom means, depending on the hour, that you'll be served hot tea and a little something sweet or a bracing cocktail and a salty snack. Whether admitting to smoking a little pot or ugly-crying over a broken heart, Mom is your girl. When you are truly shattered or the chickens have come home to roost, you never get judgment from her . . . just love.

That unconditional love, most often expressed through food, held our family together on days when it felt like we were splintering, held other people's families together though crises and trauma, and held our community together when nothing else could. Mom's food didn't come with expectations or strings; it didn't come with finger-wagging or a nickel's worth of free advice. It just invited everyone to come to the table, and then trusted the rest to us.

I see now that I could not come (back) to faith until I figured out that faith is about real hunger and real food, about the visceral reality that we are starving—for purpose, love, meaning, connection, silence, music, feasts, and fasts. I could not join a community of faith until I realized that God loves us, and calls us to love one another, because we are hobbled, imperfect creatures struggling to be something more *together*. When I came to encounter the divine in hunks of bread and bottles of wine, rather than in brittle wafers and ritual sips, found God hovering not over some hallowed altar but this dinner table, when I felt the rush of the Spirit in steam rising from a pasta pot rather than echoing in the arches of a sanctuary, then I could believe—because I had experienced it—that there was divine purpose to our being on this good earth. It is simply to love and care for one another in whatever ways we know how.

And *this girl* knows how to cook.

The truth is I'm not very good at being "spiritual." I feel silly praying alone, never knowing what to say, who to say it to, or whether anyone cares. I don't relish sitting through church services no matter how good they are. I find silent meditation roughly akin to torture. Most of the time, my mind is so full that it's only when I'm engaged in some mundane task like chopping carrots, crimping the edges of piecrust, or searing chunks of meat that my brain can finally power down. In the quietness of repetitive motion, and usually in the kitchen, I find myself in the presence of something a little bigger. I become aware of an ember of joy zinging in my chest, feel the firmness of conviction setting into my jaw, and notice the acidic burn of guilt in my throat. Without thoughts or words, I realize what makes me happy, what I need to do, where I've taken a wrong turn, or who I need to apologize to. Sometimes I just feel inexplicably whole.

Over the past few years, making bread has become the closest thing to spiritual practice I've got. Anthony and I make fresh bread a couple times a week, and when we first started, we experimented with different flours, different shapes, and different recipes. Now we use the same formula every time: six cups of flour, one cup of starter, two heaping teaspoons salt, two heaping teaspoons yeast, a dash of sugar, and enough water to transform disparate powder into smooth lastic. Whether I knead the dough by hand or stand mesmerized by the whirling dough hook on my mixer, I usually drift reverently into the ancient mystery of bread, awestruck that people have been consuming loaves of this stuff—warm out of the oven—for millennia. I find myself imagining the cave dweller who first stumbled upon wheat or contemplating the invisible miracle of yeast. If I'm making bread for someone else, I may whisper silent blessings into the mixture: happiness, peace, energy, healing, clarity.

Of course, some mornings I am so rushed that I have no time for whimsical ruminations about the history or meaning of bread. I'm lucky to get it rising while simultaneously chugging down a cup of coffee or awkwardly hopping into my skinny jeans. But on those mornings when I'm simply going through the motions, the mystery is still working its graces upon me. In an increasingly intangible, digital world, it feels powerful to make something solid, nourishing, and real. With mere yeast and water, I am able to turn cream-colored dust into voluptuous mounds of dough and then into impossibly tender yet crusty bread. I can taste it, smell it, and see it. I can slather it in Irish butter, wish over it like a birthday cake, or hand loaves of it to the men who sleep in the alley behind our church.

According to the tradition that has chosen me, when God wanted to show us how much we are loved, God became human and spent most of the time eating with people. A few nights before death came knocking, Jesus didn't sit around telling folks what to believe or who not to have sex with—he just tore a loaf of warm, dark bread into pieces and passed it around the table. When I am making bread, I understand why this is.

Because when it really matters, words alone don't cut it.

When you want someone to *know* that you love her, you have to do more than just say it. You massage her feet, unload the dishwasher, take her face in your hands and really look at her, or perhaps you share a loaf of bread and a bottle of wine, sipping out of tumblers and tearing off jagged hunks with your hands. When time is short—because your train leaves in twenty minutes or your last breath is hours away—no one wants to talk about doctrine, fix blame, or debate who is worthy of heaven. We just want to eat and remember. Maybe laugh or cry a bit. *Talking* about love—or truth or faith or beauty—only gets us so far. We need love we can touch, truth we can eat, faith we can drink, beauty we can share. What I have finally come to understand is that God wants to love us in that physical, tangible way, and that the "great commandment," summing up all religion in a sentence, enjoins us only to return that love—physically, tangibly—to God, our neighbor, and (hardest of all) ourselves.

Ultimately, it was through the physical acts of chopping, kneading, cooking, eating, and serving that I came into this most ordinary revelation. I became my own kind of Christian, and a proud one, too.

Some days, however, I am still embarrassed, though perhaps for different reasons now. I used to fret about being weird or uncool. Now mostly I am ashamed that for all our talking, singing, writing, and reading, most of us Christians don't know how to love people who are different than we are—at least not with face-holding, foot-massaging, bread-tearing love.

Despite my mortification, though, I remain what I am—a Christian. And I have come to understand, begrudgingly, a little of what those infomercial singers knew, eyes closed, swaying in that mega-church amphitheater. No matter what faith we profess, choosing to love in a community of thoroughly broken people, sharing our gifts in service of others, and living like our lives have divine purpose guarantees that we will be vulnerable to disappointment, confusion, and pain. We will love people who don't love us back, we will serve those who cannot be grateful, and we will question our existence and that of some higher being. Sometimes that vulnerability requires us to keep our eyes wide-open spying out injustice, danger, and apathy. But sometimes that exposure calls us to close our eyes and feel whatever it is that buzzes under our skin, aches in our guts, and sways unseen around us.

That day in the cafeteria, my grandparents already knew what I could not know: that school lunch with their granddaughter was the *very* place where God could be found, and for that they should give great thanks. They didn't care what a room full of elementary school-aged children thought as they said their prayer over chocolate milk and soggy sandwiches; they were about to break bread with one of God's gifts to them.

I hope one day I will have the courage to so blessedly

embarrass my grandchild in some elementary school cafeteria, but it's not likely. It will probably be that I simply bring a lunch bag full of bread, the gift of heaven and my own hands, tear off a hunk and hand it to the child, and together we will know without even knowing what wonders have passed between us.

Simple Homemade Bread

**MAKES 2 LARGE
ROUND LOAVES**

Since bread flour is expensive, I use a combination of all-purpose flour and bread flour. The starter is completely optional, but I highly recommend it. It gives the bread a more complex flavor, a darker crust, and a chewier crumb. I got my starter from a friend, but you can order it online and learn to care for it at www.kingarthurflour.com. I use instant yeast, which does not need to be activated in water. You can use the same amount of dry active yeast; just add it to the water instead of to the flour. You can make this bread in a food processor or stand mixer. You can also make it by hand if you have the time or inclination—just mix the ingredients in a bowl with a wooden spoon (or your hands!). Finally, I bake bread on unglazed quarry (terra cotta) tiles that I bought at a tile store for $7—much cheaper than an official "baking stone." If you don't have a stone or tiles, just bake the bread on a cookie sheet.

3 cups all-purpose flour

3 cups bread flour

1 tablespoon granulated sugar

2 1/2 teaspoons instant yeast (see above)

2 1/2 teaspoons table salt

1 cup sourdough starter, optional

1 3/4 cups warm water

Olive oil

In a food processor fitted with the dough blade or stand mixer fitted with the dough hook, combine the flours, sugar, yeast, salt, and starter. Turn on the machine and slowly drizzle the water into the flour mixture until the dough comes together and forms a rough ball. Add more water if the dough is too dry or more flour if it feels too wet.

Turn the dough out onto a lightly floured work surface and knead until it forms a smooth ball. Oil a large bowl with olive oil, place the dough ball in the bowl, and cover it with a damp kitchen towel or plastic wrap. Allow the dough to rise until it has at least doubled in size. (If you want a more distinct "sour" flavor, let the dough rise longer.)

When the dough has risen, turn it out onto a floured work surface and cut it in half. Working with one piece at a time, grab the edges of the dough and bring them to the center, pinching them together to form a smooth ball.

Dust a pizza peel (or cookie sheet) with cornmeal and place the dough balls pinched side down onto the peel. Make sure you set them far enough apart that they have space to rise again. Cover the dough with the same damp towel (redampen, if necessary) or more plastic wrap, and allow to rise again until doubled in size. The longer you let the bread rise the second time, the lighter and airier the crumb will be. If you like a denser bread, let it double and then bake it. If you like your bread lighter, let it triple in size before baking it.

continued on next page

While the bread is rising, heat your oven to 475°F. Adjust the rack to the lowest position and place your tiles or baking stone, if using, on the rack.

When ready to bake, use a sharp knife to slash a long, deep cut in the top of each loaf. If using a peel, quickly shimmy the dough onto the tiles and shut the oven door. If using a baking sheet, just place the sheet on the lowest rack. Bake until the crust is very dark brown, about 22 to 25 minutes. Remove the bread from the oven and transfer to a cooling rack. When the bread has cooled, store it in ziplock bags in a dry place. It should keep for about a week, more if you refrigerate it. It can also be frozen for up to 3 months.

14.

Down the Hatch,
Straight to the Heart

maggy

I
T WAS NEVER OUR INTENTION TO LIVE IN NEW YORK CITY. WHEN
we made the decision to move to the United States after our
time in Malawi, we had agreed on Boston. We needed to live
in a city for Andy's job and Boston felt manageable for two
people who had grown up in suburbia and spent the past
four years living in small-town England and a village in Africa. But with the financial crisis raging on, we had to go
where the jobs were, and Andy kept getting calls about jobs
in New York. We were resistant at first. "Not for us," we
thought. We had the same apprehension expressed by nearly
every non–New Yorker: "It's nice to visit, but I could *never*
live there." But after six weeks of living with my parents in
Connecticut, wonderful as that time was, we were ready to
be in our own place again. Andy accepted at job at an Australian investment bank in midtown. We figured a job for me
would soon follow. So we packed our U-Haul with the eight

boxes we'd shipped from England and a few pieces of hand-me-down furniture and headed for the one-bedroom apartment we'd rented on the Upper East Side.

We weren't ready for New York City. We were young and resilient, but we weren't prepared for the strains it would place on us and ultimately our young marriage. There was a year of getting acclimated; the same year in which we explored and fell in love with the bright and shiny Big Apple. But by the time we entered year two, it started to rot. Andy's job became increasingly demanding and stressful—and not just during business hours. Because he was working for an Australian company, their morning was his night and his night was their morning. He worked all day and had conference calls sometimes at 6 or 7 A.M. before he left and as many as two or three calls between 7 and 9 P.M. when he got home. There was no downtime for him. No time to unhook and unwind or to turn his mind to other important things (like me).

While Andy struggled to meet the demands of his job, I was quietly suffering at home, trying to remain positive as the reality set in that my dream job wasn't going to materialize. I had imagined that after completing my master's in international development in London, planning and fundraising for a project in Malawi, and working for several years in the nonprofit sector, I would be supremely employable. But nonprofits were suffering, making budget cuts, and downsizing personnel, and there were very few jobs available. After being rejected from positions I had applied for, I'd call to follow up and ask why I hadn't been interviewed. "We had over 300 applications including internal candi-

dates, overqualified candidates, and candidates with personal connections to the organization. Sorry." This, or some
variation, was the response nearly every time.

After a year of job hunting, I had never felt lower in my
life. The parade of "no" and the even more infuriating black
hole of résumés and cover letters sent with no response had
hollowed out my self-worth. I was cobbling together an income with a part-time, work-from-home job with a small
nonprofit and had a few freelance gigs in food, but I wanted
a *job*. After feeling down for more than a year, I craved the
routine of a nine to five and missed what it felt like to be a
valued member of a team. So when an opportunity came
along at an international association of colleges and univer-
sities, I quickly settled for a job I knew was not the right fit.
The work, though mind-numbingly boring, drained me. My
responsibilities required me to use my weaknesses, not my
strengths, leaving me very little to sustain myself or give to
others. So the job I thought would make me feel better actually made me feel worse.

It didn't take long before Andy and I were both skip-
ping breakfast and buying lunch at work. By the time I
commuted home from the job that shattered me, through
overheated subways and crowded city streets, I had no interest in cooking. I knew that I needed to, but there was
no joy in the kitchen for me anymore. Andy had other responsibilities in our household—paying bills, doing the
laundry, vacuuming—but a cook he was not. Like many
New Yorkers, we frequented restaurants and became more-
than-acquaintances with John, the guy who delivered our
sushi a couple times a week. I had the number for our local

vegetarian café programmed into my phone. When I felt guilty about getting take-out yet again, I picked up a rotisserie chicken, a baguette, cheese, prewashed salad greens in a clam shell, bottled dressing, anything that took no effort to plate up and eat in front of the television. We were eating, yes, but we were not truly being fed.

It's hard to look back on that time and know exactly what happened and why, but the result was dramatic: By the end of our second year in the city, we weren't the same loving, healthy couple we'd been for the previous eight years. We started to care less if several evenings passed where we were apart. We'd work late or meet up with friends separately and sometimes not see each other until we quietly slipped into bed. There were big fights that blew over without real resolution, the remnants of which hung heavy in the apartment like a bad smell. Simply put, we were growing apart. We could both feel the emotional chasm between us widening, but compared to the job of fixing dinner, the job of fixing our lives and our marriage felt truly impossible. So we kept drifting—for months.

Not long after that time, I read a book by nutritional psychologist Marc David, called *Nourishing Wisdom: A Mind-Body Approach to Nutrition and Well-Being*. In the book, David tells the story of a patient who suffered from many physical and emotional ailments. Desperate to feel better, the woman moved to Southern California in hopes that the balmy weather and outdoor lifestyle would improve her health. Once she arrived, she landed a job as a waitress at a vegetarian restaurant, where she worked three shifts a day.

One of the perks was that she ate three healthy, free meals while at work. To the woman's delight, her new lifestyle and diet dramatically improved her health. But after a year, her sense of well-being began to fade, so she went to see David. After hearing her story, he asked when she had last cooked a meal for herself. She admitted it had been more than a year since she had cooked anything substantial, as her meals were provided at work. He recommended nothing drastic. His only advice, "Go home and cook one meal a day for yourself. It doesn't even matter what it is." She was skeptical, as she figured her diet was already so "healthy," but she agreed to try. Within a few months her health improved dramatically, this time for good.

When I read that story a few years back, it resonated big time. I recognized that for a brief period in my life, I'd suffered from a similar affliction as the woman in David's story, and the process by which I healed was nearly the same. My lack of self-nourishment was causing deficiencies in my life, the cure was simple: Cook. And so I did.

I finally pulled together enough freelance gigs (and courage) to quit my job. While I wasn't working in international development, these jobs brought me deeper into the culinary world, consulting with food brands on social media and creating and photographing recipes for websites other than Three Many Cooks. But by that time it had become exceedingly clear to me and the people who loved me that I was a mess. The unhappiness at work had been the presenting problem, but it also meant that I wasn't doing anything for myself. I no longer found pleasure in the things I had previously cherished, namely cooking, and that ripple had rocked other parts of my life. I was ready to change—one concrete, manageable step at a time—in pursuit of healing myself and my relationship with Andy.

I made small, specific commitments: Drink at least two liters of water a day, join a gym and go three times a week, eat breakfast every morning (which I had long since stopped doing). Further, I vowed I would do one nice thing, something above and beyond, for Andy every day.

Naturally an early riser, I would set my alarm for 6:00 A.M. and head for the gym, a no-excuses time of day when I had nothing else to do. By the time I got home at 7:15, Andy would just be waking up. As he had always done, he set his alarm thirty minutes before he needed to get out of bed. Instead of pressing snooze, he slowly woke up, read the news, and checked his Blackberry.

With new commitment, I started making breakfast each morning. And so it began that my "nice thing for Andy" became delivering him a cup of tea and breakfast in bed. We're not talking frittatas and pancakes, but simple things I threw together in a few minutes like yogurt and granola or a fruit smoothie. It wasn't a huge leap to walk it into the bedroom, but those fifteen steps made an astounding difference in our relationship. I brought my coffee and bowl in, too, and sat on the bed. Suddenly, we were having a sit-down breakfast together each morning, just for ten minutes.

This small gesture brought immeasurable joy to both of us. It was a wonderful cycle, the effects of which I could not have predicted. Andy felt good first thing in the morning, I felt good for making him feel good, and we were nourished in body and soul before 7:30. After a few weeks he confessed, "Now I'm always thinking what nice little thing I can do for you in return!" He thought of many.

At first Andy did sweet, knee-jerk nice things like bringing home a giant bouquet of my favorite sunflowers or making a surprise dinner reservation at a place I wanted to try. Those grander gestures were wonderful at the start, but for the sake of sustainability he moved into smaller, more meaningful things. I'd be on a conference call in the bedroom and hear the clatter of dishes as he unloaded the dishwasher. He'd come home from work and say, "Hey gorgeous, put your shoes on! We're going for a walk around the park." The changes in our individual lives, in our marriage, in our happiness weren't gradual; they were nearly immediate. We weren't just "getting things back the way they were." We had burrowed down deeper.

I'm no fool. I know the breakfast-in-bed thing will end the moment there's a third person in our family. To everything there is a season. But this was an awakening moment when I experienced how food could heal more than just physical ailments. It holds the power to heal emotional ones, too. I was a parched plant, drooping and shriveled, but when generously doused with water, I became succulent, vibrant, and alive again.

Inspired by the healing power of a simple smoothie, dinner soon became an exciting game of "How Awesome Can I Make It Tonight?" In the winter, I labored over long-simmered sauces for pasta, homemade pizza, slow-cooked chili, and our favorite, "stoup," a hearty pot of vegetables, beans, pasta or grain, and broth whose thickness hovers somewhere between soup and stew. In the summer, I made fish tacos with slaw, meticulously wrapped summer rolls, summer squash fritters, and carefully arranged salads. I labored over dinner in the most glorious and enjoyable way, and with each meal, I could feel myself healing.

Having grown up in the Anderson household, I was well aware of the very direct correlation between food and relationships, but this powerful transformation in my young adult life, brought about by food, revealed to me the holistic way that food nourishes our spirits. This metaphysical knowledge led me to a deeper interest in the literal way that food nourishes our bodies.

Suddenly it wasn't just any food I wanted. I was hungry for the most nourishing stuff. It started with gateway health foods like kale and quinoa, and down I went, deeper and deeper into that rabbit hole, learning about everything from hemp protein and chia seeds to kohlrabi and coconut oil. Though ever-supportive, Mom and Sharon were amused by my change in diet. Admittedly, of the three of us, I had always been the most susceptible to food trends and fad diets so there were a few good-humored jabs, like placing bets on how long it would take before my new juicer was collecting dust in a closet. But I knew it was different this time because Andy and I had made the change together. We ate chard and spinach, brown rice and farro, beans and nut butters. We joined a CSA, trained for a marathon together, and started going to yoga. Through food and exercise, our lives were intertwining again, but every other area seemed to reconnect, too.

After several months of this, Andy and I agreed that we had never felt better—in body, mind, and spirit. After a year, the cumulative effect of the changes I had made was so profound that I felt completely estranged from the person I had been during that dark time. I had dropped twenty pounds, and encouraged and energized by this transformation, I added a bit of strength training to my now-daily workout. I was lively and engaged with my *self*, with Andy, with my family and friends. Slowly, it became obvious how I would move forward in my life and career. All things seemed within reach.

Hindsight is so clear. Life hands us these awful moments where we think, "Why do I have to go through this?" But then you come through the other side with deep, hard-earned wisdom that you keep forever—a worthy reward for all your trouble. Because there is not a lot of wisdom to be had without suffering, I can say that I am thankful for the dark passage. As a result, I grew not only as a cook but as a person and a partner to Andy. From young, untested love we earned our passage to the next, deeper level (of many).

These days I have a full-time job that is much better suited to me, one that draws on my skills and strengths. But when I accepted the offer I voiced my fear that, again, I would not have the will to cook when I got home at night. Mom and Sharon quickly assured me, "You're different now, Mags." And they were right. Time is certainly tighter than when I freelanced from home, but most every day I manage to get breakfast and dinner on the table, or the bed.

Now dinner preparation has become my daily joy, an eagerly anticipated moment. I sit at my desk and think about what I have at home in the fridge and pantry, fantasizing about the evening's concoction. Most nights I am home before Andy. My ritual is this: Change into pants with an elastic waist, tune into NPR's *Fresh Air*, make a martini or pour a glass of wine, and pull out my favorite cutting board and knife. Some nights I have a plan in place, other nights I don't. But there is a meditation in the peeling, dicing, slicing, stirring, searing, sautéing, and in the marrying of flavors to create a dish. It can be a quiet meditation or a lively one, but even if I'm talking to Andy instead of being silent, even if I'm listening to Usher instead of Terry Gross, even if I've got a glass of sparkling water instead of red wine, I am taking a moment to rejuvenate. It's almost as if I can feel my *self* filling up with spiritual nourishment. Because when we eat, we fill our stomachs, but when we cook, we replenish some deeper part of ourselves.

I love to anticipate that moment when Andy walks in the door, tilts back his head and, inhaling deeply, inquires "Mmm . . . what's for dinner?" I relish that moment when we sit down at the table to enjoy what I've prepared as we talk about our day. My true joy, though, is not found in the compliments or even the taste; it is present in that intangible gift of love for self and love of others.

I can hardly comprehend what dinner preparation will look like when we have kids, but I'm fairly certain it won't be a martini-in-hand meditation on a mirepoix. More than likely I'll be stealing sips of wine out of the bottle and listening to kiddie music while I throw a tray of fish sticks in the oven. There will surely be nights when boiling water and making a quick red sauce will seem a bridge too far, and on those nights there's delivery. But I know, having experienced what it is like not to cook, that I will have to find a way even when the culinary muse refuses to descend. Because a life without home-cooked food is not worth living.

Orzo, White Bean, and Kale Soup

SERVES 2 TO 3

During the winter months, this one-dish dinner is a week-night staple. I love soup, but I always wanted more of the "good stuff," so I added more stuff and less liquid to create a dish somewhere between a stew and a soup. I guess you could call it a "stoup." This orzo, white bean, and kale version is one of our favorites, but you can use almost any combination of small pasta, beans, vegetables, herbs, and spices to keep the recipe interesting. This simple recipe doesn't require home-made stock, but it certainly comes to life with it.

2 tablespoons olive oil

1 onion, cut into small dice

1 carrot, cut into small dice

1 celery stalk, cut into small dice

2 teaspoons chopped fresh rosemary

1 cup orzo

1 quart chicken or vegetable broth,
preferably homemade

1 can (15 to 16 ounces) white beans, drained

6 packed cups washed, stemmed,
and chopped kale

Heat oil in a large saucepan or a small Dutch oven over medium-high heat. Add onion, carrot, and celery; cook until soft, 5 to 7 minutes. Stir in rosemary and orzo; add broth and beans and bring to a simmer. Lower heat to medium-low and continue to cook until orzo is tender and mixture is a stewlike consistency, about 6 minutes longer. Stir in kale and cook until just wilted, a minute or 2 longer.

15.

Standing the Heat:
A Love Story

sharon

T IS IMPOSSIBLE TO TALK ABOUT MY RELATIONSHIP WITH ANTHONY without talking about food. The story of our life together is, in many ways, the story of what we have eaten.

The year we met, I was hungry.

Lost and directionless, I had gotten myself into graduate school not because I was passionate about it, but because it's what I had always said I would do. I didn't have a big dream then; I had just gotten tired of where I was and started craving something new. I fell back on an old life plan without bothering to update it: master's and PhD program in Religious Studies, and then on to teach.

The problem with going back to school, though, is that while I am really good at academic work, it is really bad for me. I am a consummate procrastinator, thriving on the pressure of last-minute deadlines to get my creativity flowing. But I am also an uncompromising perfectionist, filling every single minute until my work is due with torturous reviewing and editing. When I am backed into a corner with mere hours to the finish, I get in a zone that allows me to churn out good work, but renders me unable to think about anything other than the task at hand. I will go hours without eating, drinking, or peeing and barely notice that the sun has risen, moved across the sky, and set.

In graduate school, I had so many deadlines that this work ethic became a way of life. When I was working on a big paper, which was most of the time, I couldn't be bothered to deal with food. I would eat just enough to keep me going—a container of yogurt or a package of ramen noodles—without taking too much time away from writing. Of course, I did manage to find time to smoke cartons of cigarettes and toss back gallons of coffee to keep me buzzing. When the paper, project, or exam was finished, I would crash. Deadline adrenaline still coursing through me, I would nap fitfully before getting up, throwing on my favorite dress and heels, and heading out to celebrate over drinks with friends. Rinse. Repeat.

Because I wasn't eating much, I wasn't going to the store very often. So, even when I did have time to cook, I would open my fridge and survey my limited raw materials with a sigh. Exhausted, I couldn't muster the energy to get creative with whatever was hiding in my pantry or languishing in my crisper drawer, so I'd just grab an apple, smear it with a couple tablespoons of peanut butter, and move on. For the first time in my life, I had gotten out of the habit of feeding myself, and it showed. My clothes were starting to grow baggy, I was tired all the time, and dark smudges marred the skin beneath my eyes.

The first time I saw Anthony, we were at a student party. I was sitting on the steps with some friends, puffing on a cigarette and ignoring the food. He was a whirlwind of energy—playing Frisbee, drinking beer, eating burgers, laughing heartily. He was so vibrant—bright red T-shirt, vivid blue eyes, huge smile—I could barely look at him and yet I couldn't stop. His group of friends approached my group of friends; our eyes met with an honest-to-God zing that I felt down to my toes, but we only managed to exchange a few words before our groups headed in different directions.

When Anthony walked into my small theology seminar the following week, I felt like I had won the lottery. He plunked down in the seat right across from me and I groaned inwardly, knowing that with him sitting that close there was no way I could keep my eyes from roving over his cropped dark hair, square jaw, and a perfect dusting of stubble. Turns out, I wasn't the only one. The two of us could barely keep our eyes off each other in class, but we didn't need to since we spent most of the time verbally sparring. Good-looking *and* smart. Nice.

Anthony and I started seeing each other around campus and in class, and orchestrated study groups with mutual friends so that we could spend more time together without incurring community scrutiny. Our small, tightly knit graduate program—ostensibly populated with adults—rivaled high school in the speed and inaccuracy with which news traveled.

The weekend before our first Old Testament midterm, my roommate and I offered to host the study group at our apartment. We all agreed that involving food and wine in our cram session would make the whole process decidedly less painful, and Anthony nonchalantly piped up: "I've got some kale that's going bad in my fridge and some spent grain from home brewing in my freezer. I'll make soup and bread and bring it over." I was impressed that this guy had kale in his refrigerator *and* that he knew how to cook. Most of the guys I'd dated over the years were more the cereal, protein powder, and box macaroni and cheese types. Truth be told, though, I was more awed by Anthony's unapologetic admission that he was making us dinner with produce that was starting to go. It was so cavalier, so like my mother and so *un*like the perfectionist cook I was then.

The night of our study party, Anthony showed up at my door carrying a bright blue Dutch oven full of Caldo Verde, a Portuguese soup made with chorizo, greens, and potatoes. Some people say a man holding a puppy or a baby is irresistible. I beg to differ. There's nothing like a hot guy wearing potholders and carrying a Le Creuset full of homemade soup to get my pulse thrumming. I was practically vibrating with nervous, excited energy.

When Anthony put the pot down on my stove, I lifted the lid, inhaled the wafting steam, and felt like crying. It smelled like home—the unmistakable aroma of homemade stock, spicy sausage, and earthy greens and potatoes. My stomach clenched, and for the first time since forever I felt hungry. When I asked him if he'd made the stock himself, Anthony shrugged. "I was over at a friend's house and he was going to *throw away* the chicken carcass." He lowered his voice as if to indicate the gravity of the offense. "So, I asked if I could take it home to make chicken stock. You can't let a good carcass go to waste!" he finished with a grin. I couldn't stop the laugh that bubbled up in my throat, as I thought about how much my mom would love him. They were just two peas in an expiring-produce-reviving, chicken-carcass-loving pod.

As the group reviewed study questions and answers between gulps of wine, spoonfuls of soup, and hunks of dark, yeasty bread, I didn't feel panicked about the impending exam. Together we covered a boatload of material, ate a healthy dinner, indulged a few hilarious tangents, and broke up the party in time for us all to be in bed at a reasonable hour. Studying in community, making time for meals, and sleeping eight hours the weekend before a test were all utterly foreign to me.

That week, I found myself back in the kitchen. Dipping into good, home-cooked food had left me yearning for more real nourishment. My fridge was still empty, save a dry hunk of Parmigiano, a selection of condiments, and a few beers, so I dug around in my pantry and found a couple cans of tuna, a box of pasta, a jar of black olives, a crappy bottle of red wine, and a few cans of crushed tomatoes—relics from when my parents helped me set up my apartment. I put on my favorite Al Green album and started prepping dinner: a simple tomato sauce with tuna and olives over pasta. I poured some of the wine into the sauce and more into my glass, danced around the kitchen, belted the lyrics into my wooden spoon, and finally set a beautiful table for one. As I tucked into the first real meal I had made myself in months, it felt like there was some hope for my aching, aimless soul.

After that, things didn't get perfect, but they got better. With a little more food in me, I had energy for long runs that left my body tired enough to overrule the vortex of stress and anxiety that so often consumed my mind. I was still working like a dog, but I was smoking less and sleeping more, and that felt like a real triumph. But it wasn't just a cute boy and a healthier lifestyle that were affecting me. I was surrounded by a community of people who were so full of passion for equality, justice, faith, and love, and who seemed so sure of their role in promoting those good causes across the globe. This place, at which I had arrived with a big chip on my shoulder and without a clue, was starting to save my life. I still didn't know what I wanted to do, but I kept reading, writing, and cooking in hopes that an answer to my big question would become clear.

Meanwhile, Anthony and I debated in class, studied with friends, and chatted in the library. I was frustrated, worried that our relationship would stall out in the flirtatious friend zone. I did *not* want to be friends with him. Quietly, though, and without saying a thing to each other, we were both taking care of loose ends that needed to be tied up in order for us to start something honest and real. Anthony was in the throes of ending a long, rocky relationship, and I was working up the nerve to distance myself from a boy I couldn't get to love me but couldn't seem to get out of my system.

When Anthony finally called me one Friday afternoon and asked a little haltingly if I'd like to have dinner with him, I tried to play it cool, offering an upbeat but measured, "Sure." On my end of the phone, though, I was anything but calm. I was so excited that it felt like my chest was going to explode. As soon as I ended the call, I walked calmly out to the back porch where no one could see or hear me and let it rip. The feminist in me will die a little when I tell you that I shrieked—palms fisted, eyes squeezed shut—and jumped up and down for about thirty seconds. Having released a little of my pent-up exhilaration, I rushed back inside to get ready.

Anthony showed up, cute and confident, in a blazer and a beat-up gold minivan, which sported his mom's "I heart Boston Terriers" bumper sticker on the back. Once I had climbed gracelessly into the van, I found out that we were heading to a Salvadoran place on the other side of town. I assumed Central American food was essentially like Mexican, so I just said "Great, sounds good!" and didn't think much more about it. Though, to be honest, he could have told me that we were dining on kitty litter that night, and I wouldn't have batted an eye.

One step inside the restaurant and I knew that even my skinny jeans and little black heels were too much. There was hardly a soul in the place, save a small group of Salvadoran men in the back watching *telenovelas*. The perimeter of the room was lined with booths upholstered in shiny red plastic, and the walls were decorated with flags from the motherland and brightly colored portraits of the Virgin Mary. It smelled like pork and hot frying oil, and I was pretty sure I loved it.

When the menus arrived, it took me a second to figure

out that they were only written in Spanish. Having spent a semester in El Salvador, Anthony knew how to read the menu and what looked good, so I shrugged, smiled, and let him order for us both. I soon discovered that Salvadoran food is not like Mexican—or at least not any Mexican food I'd ever tasted. Salvadoran cuisine, which incorporates the tropical fruits, fried meats, and starchy plantains of the Caribbean with the corn and beans of Mexico, is known especially for its *pupusas*—thick corn cakes stuffed with beans, cheese, and a variety of meats and griddled to hot, pliable perfection.

Anthony ordered enough pupusas to feed us for a week. When they arrived, he showed me how to pull each one open with my fingers, top them with salsa and a pickled cabbage slaw called *curtido*, and then tear them into bite-size pieces. They tasted incredible, but the best part was getting to eat with our hands. All night long, Anthony and I drank cheap beer, gingerly handled the piping hot pupusas, and talked until they all but kicked us out.

Anthony's effect on my life was visceral. Before I met him, I was starving not only for real food but also for purpose and stability. He didn't come riding in to save me—that's not his style or mine—but he faithfully walked the road with me while I struggled to save myself. Anthony didn't force me to give up my vices or adopt his virtues; he just lived his life authentically alongside me and loved me while I figured mine out.

By the time we were ready to debut our relationship to my parents, Anthony and I were a force to be reckoned with in the kitchen. We were cooking together most meals of the day, and our tasty triumphs were making us bold. Anthony was challenging me to try new things and teaching me the great secrets of Italian cooking learned at his father's elbow. I was schooling him in knife skills and classic cooking techniques and introducing him to the flavors of India and the Far East.

As we started planning that first family gathering, my brave boyfriend assented to meeting everyone at once— Mom, Dad, Maggy, and Andy. Knowing he'd be more comfortable doing something, rather than sitting on a stool with a glass of wine and getting interrogated, Anthony suggested that we cook dinner for my family. We'd been perfecting a coffee- and chipotle-braised pulled pork recipe, so we settled on that as filling for tacos. We rounded out the menu with homemade corn tortillas and loads of fresh toppings: guacamole, queso fresco, chopped cabbage and cilantro, Mexican crema, lime wedges, pickled onions, and three different salsas—pico de gallo, salsa verde, and fiery habañero sauce. Anthony, a budding mixologist, volunteered to make authentic margaritas, and I took on dessert, a sweet and spicy Mexican chocolate ice cream.

We gathered our recipes, made a long shopping list, and hit up all the local Latin markets to find the most authentic ingredients. While browsing the produce aisle, Anthony jokingly started poking me with a long, crooked yucca and waggling his eyebrows suggestively. Then he got serious and said, "Hey, we should fry this up as an appetizer—it's really good with a mojo sauce." I knew my mom wouldn't say no to anything fried, so we bought the yucca and a bunch of green plantains to turn into über-crispy vehicles for that citrusy, garlicky sauce.

That afternoon, Anthony and I packed up our car with *way* too much food, booze, pots, pans, and cooking utensils for one night, and drove the forty-five minutes south along Interstate 95 to my parents' place. We arrived in their kitchen, arms heavily laden with ingredients, and everyone jumped up to help and tried valiantly to pretend they weren't sizing up my new boyfriend. Of course, when Anthony turned around to mix drinks, all four of them started giving me big, exaggerated winks and thumbs-up.

There was a lot of work to do, and Anthony figured that if we let my family sit on their butts drinking margaritas, then we wouldn't eat until 10 P.M. So, he started assigning roles. "Pam, you're Southern, so you know how to fry things, right? How 'bout you take care of this yucca and the plantains?" he said. Sizing up my dad and pegging him as more a doing-the-dishes guy, Anthony put him to work juicing limes for more drinks and cleaning up after everyone. Sympathizing with the newbie, Andy saw guacamole ingredients and offered to take on that project, while I showed Maggy how to shape and press the tortillas and griddle them until warm and speckled brown. Once everyone was working, Anthony turned his attention to the mojo and salsas and finished the meat, and I sliced cabbage and cilantro, crumbled cheese, and made the custard base for our chocolate-chile ice cream. At one point, I looked up from the stove where I was infusing chocolate with spices and dried chiles and saw everyone gathered around the island working intently on their assigned projects, sipping their margaritas, and laughing. There was no two ways about it: Anthony fit. Anyone who could mix a stiff drink, cook like a pro, and take charge of our motley crew was going to be just fine.

When we finally sat down to eat, my dad asked Anthony to pray *in Spanish.* I was so mortified that I nearly crawled under the table. But Anthony didn't miss a beat. If I hadn't already been in love with him, I would have fallen ass over applecart when he grabbed the hands next to him, bowed his head, closed his eyes, and murmured a beautifully incomprehensible (to me) prayer. I knew he'd passed my mom's test by standing the Anderson family heat in our kitchen, but as we all lifted our heads and opened our eyes, I could tell that he had also impressed my father. Maggy and Andy were easier to please—the meal turned out so well that they were pretty much sold on the spot.

Anthony and I were lucky to figure out quickly and easily that food is, as often as not, the language of our love. We say those three little words plenty, but just as regularly we enact those words by cooking with and for each other. I always joke that when something is wrong in our relationship it means we've haven't made enough food or enough love lately. It's funny, of course, because it is *so* true. Getting into bed or into the kitchen helps repair our neglected connection, not only because both activities are fun but also because these things require trust, communication, and teamwork. We have come to understand and take seriously the fact that cooking is an essential part of our relationship. The food is important, but it's the time together that really nourishes us.

People are always asking where Anthony and I find so

much time to cook. I tell them the answer is simple: at this point in our lives, it is absolutely our number one priority. Rarely are we trying to avoid or rush through cooking to get to some other event or activity. For some people, cooking is a means to an end, but for us it is the main event. Anthony and I cook because we love it, but we also cook because we need it. Our bodies, our lives, and our relationship just don't work right without cooking. If we ever decide to switch jobs or have children, that may change, but I doubt it. Something tells me Anthony and I will be cooking, eating, dancing, drinking, and, yes, fighting in our kitchen until death do us part.

Caldo Verde

(PORTUGUESE SAUSAGE, GREENS, AND POTATO SOUP)

MAKES ABOUT 4 QUARTS

This is the deliciously rich and earthy soup that Anthony brought to my house for that first, fateful study group meal. It's a great way to use up withering greens—but I should warn you, it can have the unforeseen side effect of making people fall in love with you. Caldo Verde is heavenly when made with homemade stock and dried beans. Though soaking and cooking dried beans take advance preparation, the deep flavor the beans acquire while simmering in the soup is unmatched by their canned cousins. If you don't have time for dried beans, just drain and rinse two 15-ounce cans of white beans and add them to the soup with the potatoes.

1 1/2 cups dried white beans, such as cannellini or Great Northern

1 pound (about 4 links) fresh Andouille or Spanish chorizo (pork sausage)

1 large onion, diced

3 medium celery stalks, diced

2 medium carrots, diced

Kosher salt and black pepper

5 medium garlic cloves, minced

1 tablespoon tomato paste, preferably double concentrated

continued on next page

2 bay leaves

1 1/2 teaspoons pimentón (smoked paprika)

1/2 teaspoon dried thyme leaves

1/4 to 1/2 teaspoon crushed red pepper flakes, to taste

1 1/2 cups dry white wine

4 cups low-sodium chicken stock, preferably homemade

4 cups cold water

1 1/2 pounds firm potatoes, such as red or Yukon gold, cut into bite-size chunks

1 very large bunch of kale or collard greens, washed and roughly chopped

1 teaspoon sherry or red wine vinegar

Olive oil

Chopped fresh parsley, for garnish

Place the dried white beans in a large bowl and generously cover with cold water. Allow the beans to soak, adding more water if necessary, for 8 hours or overnight.

In a large Dutch oven or soup kettle over medium heat, cook the sausage links until firm, adding a little olive oil to the pan if the sausage sticks. Once the sausage is done, remove it from the pot and slice each link into bite-size pieces.

If the sausage has given off a good amount of fat, remove all but 2 tablespoons. If not, add enough olive oil to equal 2 tablespoons. Increase the heat under the Dutch oven to medium-high. Add the onions, celery, carrots, 2 teaspoons of kosher salt, and a few grinds of black pepper. Sauté, stirring occasionally, until the vegetables are soft, 5 to 8 minutes. Stir in the garlic, tomato paste, bay leaves, pimentón, thyme, red pepper flakes, and sausage, and cook until the spices are fragrant and the tomato paste begins to darken, another 2 to 3 minutes.

Add the white wine and cook, stirring occasionally, until the wine has reduced by half. Add the chicken stock and 4 cups of cold water, and bring to a boil. Reduce to a simmer and taste the soup, seasoning with additional salt, pepper, and spices if necessary.

Drain the soaked beans, and add them to the pot. Simmer the soup, stirring occasionally, until the beans are nearly tender, about 45 minutes. Add the potatoes and continue cooking until the beans and the potatoes are barely tender, another 10 to 15 minutes.

To give the soup nice body and texture, ladle 2 cups of soup into a food processor or blender, and process until smooth. Return this liquid to the Dutch oven and simmer for another 5 minutes.

Turn off the heat and, once more, season to taste with salt and pepper. Add the greens and the vinegar; stir to combine. Cover and let stand until the greens are bright and tender, but not overcooked, about 5 minutes. Garnish with parsley and serve with crusty bread.

16.

No Partiality

pam

WHEN IT CAME TO MAGGY AND SHARON, MY MOM'S mantra was "I don't want to show no partiality," which we all knew was her perpetual reminder *not* to favor Maggy, with whom she had a special bond. Fortunately Papa, a second child too, had a soft spot for Sharon, so things evened out.

Growing up, Maggy and Sharon frequently complained that the other was my favorite, which I took as a good sign. There are times when I feel closer to one, or more in sync with the other, but I love, respect, and delight in both of my two very different daughters.

When they were young, their differences were writ large. Maggy, a Taurus, was bold and fearless. Her second-grade teacher predicted she would be the first woman president. Maggy was also a little naïve. For fear she'd be made fun of in school, I finally had to tell my eight-year-old (Maggy swears she was ten) there wasn't really a Santa. Even then she set her jaw and persisted in her battered belief.

When it came to parties, Maggy loved splashy bashes—her birthdays were notoriously large and high-concept. Still are, actually. Her thirtieth birthday party found forty of her closest friends at a sit-down dinner in my living room (from which I emptied most of the furniture to make room for the tables), causing a few guests to observe that this fete was slightly more elaborate than the last small wedding they'd attended.

Maggy skimmed her homework and was done. She viewed long-term assignments as group projects and would wrangle in family, friends, teachers—whoever could help deliver the best. Like her tenth-grade science fair project on sourdough bread. Maggy's genius was getting me to suggest a topic I'd be interested in. I fed those starters more faithfully than she did (of course). We were both proud the night her project placed at the regional competition.

Growing up, Maggy loved her family, but she didn't especially love being home. All that changed in 2001. It was Labor Day weekend, and we were at Kenyon College. I could hardly wait and hardly stand to drop her off. It had been a difficult summer, and we weren't sure if she would make it in college, but the truth is, we weren't sure she could make it at home anymore—or that *we* could. Just twelve days later the Twin Towers tumbled, and Maggy used all of that strong will of hers to find someone driving our way and hitched a seven-hour ride home for a very short weekend. She had left us just days before as a brooding teen and so quickly returned a frightened young woman. But, all the same, a woman.

Sharon was brainy, pensive, and a touch shy, oftentimes the teacher's pet. As a young girl she fell periodically into odd fixations. For weeks she would wear a white jersey slip—no dress—to preschool every day, and for a solid year she ate only macaroni and cheese for lunch. She had a reputation as a biter.

Early on Sharon was one of those rare disciplined students who'd start work on a project the day it was assigned and diligently plug away until completion, her work perfectly timed with the due date (in high school she started to become more of a procrastinator). She might consult with others along the way, but she was mostly content to work on her own.

Her birthday parties were interesting and low-key. She'd plan a great menu (it was always about the food) and then invite a few good friends. For her tenth birthday we hosted a murder mystery dinner. One year she and her guests cooked her dinner, complete with a sparkler-topped croquembouche-style cupcake tree. Another year a few of us went strawberry picking and made pies.

As soon as Maggy left home and Sharon didn't have to play little sister anymore, she became the adult she had always wanted to be. Instead of the four of us going to *Spiderman* at the local multiplex, the three of us would see *Talk to Her* at the local arts theater. At dinner we played classical music and discussed *The Great Gatsby* or Joseph Campbell's *The Power of Myth.*

The only thing Sharon needed from me was a kick in the pants to apply for college. Despite her great prospects of attending a top school, Sharon approached the whole process with such a lack of enthusiasm I was convinced she'd miss the deadline, end up at home another year, and in the process lose her drive. Once she got wait-listed at her early-decision first choice, she lost all interest.

It was hard for me to play the role of a hands-on demanding parent since my child now self-identified as an adult, but I did. As a result she moved from wait-listed to accepted at her first choice school. A few years later she confessed to me that what paralyzed her was pure fear of rejection. I'm glad I didn't let my anger and frustration at what appeared to be cocky nonchalance get in the way of my helping her get what she deeply wanted but was too afraid to pursue.

There was no confusing Maggy and Sharon for each other as kids, but now that they are young adults some think they're fraternal twins. I don't see it. As they have grown into women, much of the youthful exaggeration that proclaims, "I'm different!" has faded into maturity, but Maggy and Sharon are still a study in contrasts. Take our squabbles, for example.

My fights with Maggy are fiery hot and tornado-like. With very little warning and seemingly out of nowhere they whip up quickly and escalate fast. All of a sudden it's scary, and I wonder how our relationship will ever survive such a violent verbal whirlwind. And then as quickly as it starts, it's over, and we peacefully pick up the pieces and learn for next time.

A few months ago Maggy and I were together for one of our regular food photography shoots. It was a great day, but by midafternoon we were both getting a little testy. When

Maggy said "Absolutely not" to the red plaid napkin I had chosen for the final tilapia shot, I should have recognized that conditions were ripe for a fight, but I couldn't resist. I shot back, "I've been in this business for nearly thirty years, but working with you, you'd think I didn't know a damn thing about food styling." A short, volatile exchange ensued. Maggy quickly threw her bag together, walked the two miles to the station, and caught the next train back to New York. Before she had even found her seat I texted, "Where are you?" and she immediately responded. With that I called, and we talked her entire hour-long train ride back, poking fun at our silly selves.

Fighting with Sharon, on the other hand, is more like a polar vortex. Since we don't live near each other, our relationship is phone- and Internet-dependent, so it's easy to settle in for the big chill. Fights usually start with a hang-up, followed by a long deep freeze. After days of dead quiet and soul-chilling temperatures, Mother Nature intervenes and there's a thaw. Slowly the crocuses and snowdrops push through, and it's spring again.

I think of the time I scolded Sharon for saying "yes" to everyone (and the implied "no" to Maggy and me). As usual, she hung up. I let it go a few days and then tested the ice by sending a friendly, but strictly work-related e-mail. No answer. Another few days passed, and I sent a warm motherly text. No response. Coincidentally, I would be driving through Atlanta in a few days, and before our fight we had discussed getting together for lunch. The night before, I texted again to confirm our lunch date. Radio silence. I was upset. How could she be so cold?

David suggested I leave her alone, but how could I possibly pass through Atlanta, where she and Anthony had recently moved, and not see my daughter? A few hours out I called. Still no answer. But in a few minutes she returned the call—she had been in the shower. The conversation was chilly until it became clear she had forgotten I was passing through town. Thinking my text was a reminder for a lunchtime phone meeting, she had ignored it. I was so shaken and relieved she was not spitefully ignoring me that I started to cry, which broke the ice. What followed that day was a long, profound mother-daughter lunch.

The girls' weddings were also a reflection of their very different personalities. Maggy and Andy's 275-guest gala was an all-out community effort at our home during an August heat wave, while Sharon and Anthony's—a thoughtful service and well-planned menu for close family and friends—fell on a frosty Saturday the week before Christmas.

I often tell the story of how Maggy *had* to get married, and everyone laughs. But the fact is that if Maggy, a twenty-three-year-old American woman, and Andy, a twenty-four-year-old Englishman, wanted to live in the same country, they had to get legal. Some were skeptical but David and I weren't worried. We had married straight out of college and found that we loved being young enough to enjoy our life post-children.

Still, Maggy *was* young. She had just graduated from university in England and had come back to the States to work a year before her wedding. After that, she and Andy would move to England. For how long she did not know. Living at home, loving home (and a good party), and knowing she would soon leave it all, she wanted a big church wedding with a tented outdoor reception in our backyard, which was very possible since we lived in a lovely rectory next door to a beautiful church. Her father a long-time priest, her mother a veteran caterer, the talents of two entire church communities in Solebury and Darien, a host of family and friends— she had a built-in wedding team ready to help pull off her big bash. So we could be mother and father of the bride, David turned the wedding ceremony over to his minister brother, Michael, and I hired a caterer to supplement my menu and serve the event.

As a nod to Andy's English roots (and quite practically to keep people from getting too happy too soon), we offered teatime during picture time. I would make bars and brownies to fill out the table but our former church in Solebury, Pennsylvania, agreed to bake hundreds of their beautifully decorated Trinity Cookies, a seventy-year-old Christmas tradition revived in July just for Maggy.

From there guests would walk the path from the church to our tented backyard where we'd start with big platters of deviled eggs, along with bowls of rosemary-scented Union Square Café–Inspired Bar Nuts, our family's signature cocktail fare for years.

Our young groom may have been English but he loved all things American, and he and Maggy were agreed. It would be a traditional barbecue feast—pulled pork, baked beans (one of Andy's top-ten favorites), classic potato salad, coleslaw, and corn muffins. That's what I could pull off ahead. The rest—barbecued chicken, tomato–red onion salad, peach cobbler, and the cupcake tree—we'd leave to the caterer.

My goal was to take off my apron Thursday afternoon and be Maggy's mom for the weekend, and thanks to the help of my friend Terrie and my sisters-in-law Jeanne and Susan, we were right on schedule. Before heading off to Thursday night's party I walked the caterers to the over-size refrigerator and freezer in the church kitchen and proudly showed them our meal, beautifully organized, prepped to perfection. They'd take over from here, assembling the dishes and serving our big crowd.

In keeping with her personality, Maggy's bachelorette party was splashy, too. Thursday night before the wedding the bridesmaids and aunts, a smattering of family women friends, Andy's mother, and I—twenty of us in all— launched from the Norwalk Maritime Center in a pontoon boat loaded with a case of rosé champagne. The summer evening cruise took us over Long Island Sound, and the cool water breezes were a perfect answer to the August heat. We landed on Sheffield Island, where we feasted on steamed lobsters and mussels, potatoes, and corn. After a week of hard kitchen labor, it felt good to let go a little—to eat, drink, and let the magic happen. The boat docked at the end of the night and we all parted ways, the younger set heading out for a few hours of dancing, the rest of us hoping for a few hours of deep sleep.

Friday night the summer fever broke, and we woke to a near-cool summer Saturday. As I woke in our peaceful home, I was grateful for friends in town who had housed the bridal party and so many of our family members. Everywhere we walked on Saint Luke's campus, there were bustling signs of the big day ahead. When I walked into the church kitchen I was indebted to everyone who had worked all week helping prepare our barbecue buffet. When I opened the church office and saw buckets and buckets of flowers parishioners had so generously cut from their gardens, I was overwhelmed. Then I looked up and saw the host of Altar Guild women transforming them all—peonies, lilies, sunflowers, delphiniums, hydrangeas, sunflowers, and more—into glorious centerpieces. I was giddy with gratitude.

And Saturday afternoon as I was flipping burgers on the deck watching all the energetic young people setting up the tables and chairs for the reception, I was grateful again. I passed my four sisters-in-law in the church cloisters cutting and arranging bars for the post-wedding tea, and—as an only child—I felt blessed to have real sisters. When I accepted the tins filled with Trinity cookies as our Solebury, Pennsylvania, friends were stepping off their chartered bus, I felt their love.

Shortly before the ceremony I heard the pickup choir comprised of so many of our family and friends as they practiced "Praise My Soul the King of Heaven." If my adrenaline hadn't been so elevated, I would have cried. The service was magnificent, the reception electric, and not because they were lavish, but because nearly everyone there had helped make it happen. It took a village.

There was always an assumption that I would cater Sharon's wedding. Over the years she and I would spend hours on long walks planning her fantasy wedding, particularly the menu. It changed frequently, but it was always classy winter comfort—osso bucco with saffron risotto, fork-tender lamb shanks, rich beef stew, roasted root vegetables, big stinky cheese and charcuterie boards. Oysters! We envisioned a backyard tent, but it'd have to be heated because while her menu might change, the wedding was always at Christmas.

Once Sharon and Anthony met at Yale Divinity School they found a new community, and when they set out to plan their wedding it was clear: They should be married in their community at the school's colonial-style Marquand Chapel. We tried to figure out how I could cater a reception forty-five minutes from home in the dead of winter. Every time we strategized, it felt complicated and stressful. When I was finally relieved of my duties, I was free to give myself to this wedding.

Sharon and Anthony quietly and diligently worked together to plan a meaningful wedding that reflected their beliefs. For starters, there was no flashy diamond engagement ring. They each wore a wooden band until their wedding day when they replaced them with ones made from reclaimed metal: Anthony's palladium, Sharon's rose gold.

Maggy threw Sharon's bachelorette party right at our Bucks County home on a beautiful fall weekend. Maggy, Sharon, and the rest of the bridesmaids spent a quiet weekend making homemade pizza, hiking the Appalachian Trail, and touring craft breweries. There might have been a night out to tie one on, but I never heard anything about it.

Not having to prepare the big wedding feast freed me up to have fun and to be a good host on different turf. The day

before the wedding I reserved a local nail salon and organized a champagne-sushi lunch, and at Saturday's hair salon
session I ordered sandwich trays for the bridal party and the
family and friends who stopped by.

After the wedding rehearsal on Friday night we de-
camped to New Haven's famous Pepe's Pizza. We sat on rick-
ety chairs at beat-up tables (Pepe's is all about the pies, not
the décor) and sampled slices of Margherita and their signature white clam sauce, then more unusual varieties like
white pizza with spinach, mushrooms, and Gorgonzola.
When the chef invited us into the kitchen to make our own
pie, I was first in line to wield the eight-foot pizza paddle
and shove my shrimp, bacon, and spinach round into the
blazing brick oven.

Sharon and Anthony subscribed to the modern belief
that the bride's family should not shoulder the cost of the
entire wedding. Better yet, Anthony's parents shared their
conviction. Who were we to argue with anyone's sincere belief? So the four parents tallied the weekend's expenses and
split it down the middle. In that same spirit, Anthony came
into the chapel holding his mother on one arm and his father on the other, and when it was time for the bride to come
down the aisle, both David and I together walked our daughter to the altar.

Reflecting Sharon and Anthony's commitment to eating
sustainably, seasonally, and locally, their reception was catered farm-to-table. Instead of traditional late-summer rata-
touille, their winter version was made with hearty root
vegetables. A big pot of ham-hock-braised kale took the

place of the ubiquitous salad. The braised chicken thighs were free-range, alongside a gigantic bowl of Sharon's beloved mac and cheese.

The wedding cake was savory—three beautiful tiers of Cypress Grove cheese. For dessert we delivered oversized plates of sweets to each table, compliments of Anthony's Italian grandmother who made hundreds of pizzelles. I contributed to the plate too, baking up lime bars, cream cheese–frosted cranberry brownies, peppermint bark, linzer cookies, and biscotti. At the end of the night the veteran wedding photographer told Sharon and Anthony it was the most beautiful and eloquent wedding service he had ever witnessed and asked for a copy of the liturgy to share with future clients.

I'll never forget the guest at Maggy's wedding who commented that my potato salad wasn't salted enough and the corn muffins were a tad dry. I agreed and responded with a smile, "I can be in the kitchen and make it perfect, or I can be out here and enjoy my daughter's wedding." Frankly, I'd give the food at both weddings a solid B, but at the end of each night, David and I knew we had just experienced the best, proudest days of our lives.

As for a favorite, I'm certain that each of the girls think I liked her wedding best.

Smokey Oven-Barbecued Pork

SERVES 16 TO 20

Along with the caterer's barbecued chicken, Smokey Oven-Barbecued Pork was the main course I made for Maggy and Andy's wedding. It's a great recipe for serving a crowd, because from roasting to pulling to saucing, it's completely make-ahead. You can skip the smoking step, but the flavor the pulled pork absorbs with just 15 minutes on the grill is remarkable. For an equally good taco filling, add a couple of tablespoons of cumin to the spice rub.

3 tablespoons brown sugar

3 tablespoons paprika

1 1/2 tablespoons coarsely ground
     black pepper

1 1/2 tablespoons garlic powder

1 1/2 teaspoons salt

1 bone-in pork shoulder butt roast or
     1 fresh picnic shoulder (8 to 9 pounds)

1/2 cup Dijon mustard

3 cups wood chips, such as hickory
     or mesquite

Adjust oven rack to lowest position and heat oven to 250°F. Mix the brown sugar, paprika, pepper, garlic, and salt in a small bowl. Pat the roast dry and place on a rack over a foil-lined shallow pan. Lightly sprinkle the top and sides of the roast with salt,

continued on next page

brush with half the mustard, then sprinkle with half the spice rub. Carefully turn roast over and repeat with a little salt and remaining mustard and spice rub. (Can be covered and refrigerated a couple of days.)

Place pork in the oven; roast until a meat thermometer registers 170°F, 9 to 11 hours, depending on roast's size and internal temperature at the start of cooking. Transfer roast to a platter and let cool enough to handle, about 1 hour.

Meanwhile, place chips in a small bowl; fill bowl with water to completely cover; let stand 15 to 20 minutes. If making sandwiches or if pork needs a little more moisture, pour off any fat and scrape pan drippings into a small saucepan, add 1 cup of water, and bring to a simmer. Cut pork roast into 1- to 2-inch chunks and shred into disposable tin.

Remove rack or racks from a gas grill. Lay a large sheet of heavy-duty foil the size of the grill over the burners. Carefully puncture the foil all over with a fork. Scatter drained chips over foil. Set grill racks back in position; close grill lid. Turn all burners on high and heat grill until the first wisps of smoke from the smoldering chips appear. Place pan of pulled pork on the grill. Close lid, reduce heat to medium-high, and smoke until grill stops smoking, about 15 minutes. Add the pork-flavored liquid (and barbecue sauce, if you like); stir to combine. Serve! (Pork can be covered and refrigerated for several days.)

New and Improved Peppermint Bark

MAKES ABOUT 2 DOZEN PIECES

New and Improved Peppermint Bark is one of the many sweets I made for Sharon and Anthony's Christmastime wedding. I use chocolate graham crackers for crunch, which also makes this confection just as irresistible, but with a tad fewer calories.

If you can't find the candy cane Kisses in the store, substitute with 2 ounces of chopped white chocolate and 12 crushed peppermint candies (to do this, place in a sealed bag and crush with a rolling pin).

12 chocolate graham crackers

6 tablespoons butter

1/4 cup sugar

4 ounces white chocolate, chopped

4 ounces bitter- or semi-sweet chocolate, chopped

4 ounces (about 24) candy cane Kisses, chopped

Adjust oven rack to lower-middle position and heat oven to 350°F. Grease a 9 × 13-inch rimmed baking sheet with vegetable cooking spray. Line pan bottom and up and over the long sides with heavy-duty foil for easy removal. Grease foil with vegetable

continued on next page

cooking spray and then line with crackers, sugar side down, cutting as necessary to fit pan.

Heat the butter and sugar in a small saucepan over medium heat, stirring frequently, until simmering. Pour mixture evenly over crackers and working quickly, use a spatula to spread it.

Bake until bubbly and golden brown, about 10 minutes. (Watch carefully to make sure it doesn't burn.) Remove from oven and sprinkle both white and dark chocolate over hot crackers; let stand a few minutes and spread the chocolate with the back end of a spoon (or finger if you can stand the heat) in figure eights, creating a marbleizing effect. Sprinkle with Kisses. Freeze until firm.

Using the heavy-duty foil handles, remove bar from pan. Break into pieces and serve.

17.

In Her Apron

maggy

MUST LOOK LIKE AN IDIOT. I AM CARRYING FOUR CANVAS BAGS whose sturdy, fortified seams are actually straining against the weight of the groceries they struggle to hold. I'm making my way from our Upper West Side apartment to Dad and Mom's house in Connecticut, first by subway, then by train. These bags hold the essential ingredients of our traditional Christmas Eve feast.

"Who does this, Maggy?" I ask myself, as I stop to adjust the straps cutting into my shoulder. A normal person carting this much stuff would get a cab. Actually, a normal person would be smart enough to get to Connecticut and *then* grocery shop. "Who does this?" The question returns. I know the answer: "Pam Anderson's daughter does this."

It's December 23, 2012. Mom is in Panama City, Florida, with her parents, and Sharon and Anthony are celebrating their first Christmas in Atlanta. While many of our family's fondest memories are of Christmas celebrations with our grandparents, those days are long gone. Their last Christmas with us up North was in 2009. That year, a combination of their advanced age and a wicked freeze sent them both into some hacking, wheezing illness that leveled them for weeks. In Granny's case, months. To this day, Mom sees that Christmas as the beginning of the end for them.

This isn't Mom's first year going down to Florida for Christmas. As an only child, she felt honor-bound to be with her parents and provide cheer now that they had so little to celebrate. In her absence, Sharon and Anthony would come down from New Haven, where they were studying, and Andy and I would come out from the city for a low-key celebration with Dad.

But with Sharon in Atlanta, there is only me this year. Andy and I had considered having Christmas Eve in the city with some friends. Since the Eve is a big workday for Dad, our real Christmas celebration comes on Boxing Day. Mom would be back from Florida, and we'd be together then. But I didn't like the idea of Dad being on his own. Neither did Mom. Christmas Eve is relentless and exhausting for an Episcopal priest and frustrating for his family. We got through it by sticking together, so leaving him alone didn't seem right.

When I called Dad to talk about our plans, he said we should stay in the city and enjoy ourselves. He meant it, too. With such a grueling day ahead, he said, "I wouldn't mind coming home, heating up some leftovers, and heading to bed." But Mom and I knew better. Dad's Christmas Eve started at 3 P.M. and ended well after midnight with six services and a loony pageant in between.

The long day of Christmas Eve prep was always punctuated with Dad's presence. He'd pop home in between services, close the door to his office, and practice his sermon or write the text for announcements, but not without stopping by the kitchen to cut off the edge of a honey-glazed ham or snatch a mini biscuit off a baking sheet. Mom would give him a meaningless slap on the wrist, then make him a sandwich or heat a bowl of leftover soup. He would retreat up the back staircase with his little prize. These were short but important interactions. Like the month of Advent culminating in Christmas, this long day was redeemed by the celebration at the end. Dad slogged on knowing someone was home preparing a midnight party. The house would be oven warmed. There would be food. Champagne. There would be loved ones and a few close friends, laughter and off-color jokes. The thought of him confecting Christmas for thousands and coming home this year to an empty house was not acceptable. I insisted I host Christmas Eve at Mom and Dad's house.

Our family friends who had shared this tradition with us for almost a decade were happy to hear I'd be picking up the torch—or whisk—and offered to help me. Could I pull it off? I had lived the tradition for almost twenty years, but did that mean I could do what my mother had done? I was the elf suddenly promoted to Santa.

Over those twenty years, Sharon and I had tasks that increased from cosmetic to critical. We took great delight in festively decorating the kitchen island with found objects we'd dig out from around the house. We spent hours creating signs for the food and artfully arranging champagne flutes on trays, debating the merits of each potential tablecloth that might serve as the base for the all-important tablescape.

In the days when we still wore matching Hanna Andersson dresses, it would be the Twelve Days of Christmas tablecloth gilded with repurposed, multicolor table confetti and the nubs of pink Advent candles from years past in gaudy crystal candelabras. In the years when you wouldn't catch us wearing even the same pair of socks, the decorations got more tasteful. The antique-white tablecloth with understated candles embroidered at the edges, adorned with fresh-cut greens, tea lights in glass votives, and white Christmas lights draped dramatically across the island.

Wanting to keep us involved even after the table decorating was complete, Mom would task us with finding the appropriate serving dish for each item on the menu. We, her eager elves, would head down to the basement, where the seasonal dishes lived 364 days a year: the extra-large Santa Claus platter large enough for several pounds of lemon chicken wings, the Christmas tree dish just right for a few cups of Mom's spiced mixed nuts, and the long, slender, leaf-shaped tray that perfectly displayed the miniature crab cakes every year.

As soon as we had enough muscle to transfer a seven-quart Dutch oven from stove to sink, we were given work that was actually useful and carried out with considerably less delight. We would load the dishwasher, scrub pans, or wipe down the "horizontal surfaces" as Dad called them. Eventually we developed our knife skills and could chop, dice, and slice anything Mom put in front of us.

Once I could drive, Sharon and I would make runs to the store for last-minute must-haves. I rejoiced each time Mom discovered a missing ingredient. I got to drive, and, when we got to the Stop & Shop, I would send Sharon in for the powdered sugar and currants while I stole a cheeky cigarette out back.

We did whatever Mom asked because with each passing year, we grew increasingly aware that despite Mom's status as a culinary badass, this was still a massive undertaking and our roles were key if not to the night's success, then to ensuring Mom's sanity.

Some years were easier to pull off than others, but no matter: At 5:00 P.M. you would find Mom in a classy, conservative dress hovering over the stove in her slippers—makeup and pantyhose on, earrings and rollers in. The commercial-grade exhaust fan whirring on high, drowning out *Festival of Carols,* which sang from the stereo. With all four burners on medium-high and two roasting pans side by side, each over two burners to provide maximum surface area to fry, sauté, and sear the last-minute appetizers in large batches, Mom could knock out the hot stuff in twenty minutes flat.

This was one of probably four times a year when Mom, who cooked three meals a day, every day, considered an apron necessary (and her stained, singed everyday wardrobe showed it). But on this night, she wanted to be as ready as she could by 5:30. The frying needed to be done at the last minute, so all dressed and aproned she'd be pulling spring rolls out of bubbling, spattering oil, transferring them to wire racks over newspaper. Even with the apron, it still felt precarious. Like a bulletproof vest, there was still so much exposed!

Most years, the Christmas Eve smorgasbord felt like it wouldn't come together in time. But for a woman whose watchword was always "care deeply without caring at all," Mom didn't really mind if people turned up to a slight mess or a party already on the go. No matter. It was always "fine" by the time the first gleeful guests knocked on the tiny glass window of our side door bearing bubbly, gifts, and dishes to add to the spread.

Some years Mom, Sharon, and I would be perched on stools or sitting on the counter, tucking into our first well-deserved drink, nibbling at the crispy, caramelized edges of a lemon chicken wing, or trying vainly to cover the evidence of a seriously depleted bowl of pimento cheese.

Other years, the feast would be ready, but we'd all be up-stairs putting the finishing touches on ourselves when we'd hear the telltale suction-open, slam-close of the side door. Mom would shout down the hall from her bathroom to ours, where Sharon was doing my eye makeup, "Girls! One of you go downstairs!" Her tone wasn't panicked, it was matter of fact. Ready or not we'd go, mascara on one eye, because by God that woman deserved an extra five minutes to get ready. And when, just minutes later, she did come down, looking like the First Lady ready for a *Vanity Fair* cover shoot, our guests practically applauded. Drinks were poured, hot food was transferred from a warm oven to platters, plastic wrap was removed from room-temperature dishes, and the party began.

AND SO, AS I RIDE THE Metro-North train bound for Mom and Dad's house in Darien, I am reliving the scene I am supposed to re-create. I make a mental list of what I need to do and when: Decide on the menu well in advance, make a shopping list, shop the day before (which is why I am a pack mule riding a train), make anything possible in advance, get the table set long before guests arrive, chill the booze once there's space in the fridge, get yourself mostly ready, finish cooking off the hot stuff, care completely without caring at all, enjoy your own party.

The next morning I start by making Dad breakfast. Like Mom. Eggs over easy on toast. She always wanted him to have something hearty to fortify him for the day ahead. He's delighted, surprised. He smiles, scarfs, and he's out the door. I'm straight into mega-prep and relieved that I've already shopped.

Still, I call Mom no less than a dozen times. "How far in advance can I fill the deviled eggs?" "Should I use the glazing goop that comes with the ham?" "Can I sub peppers for olives?" "Where do you keep your cornstarch?" Patiently she answers each question.

I follow the instructions, and though it is not 5:30, I am in my dress, my hair done (if slightly damp at the temples and neck), makeup and tights on, shoeless, hovering over the stove with two sauté pans and two Dutch ovens, all blazing and bubbling away. Friends arrive, someone hands me a drink, and I simultaneously fry potato pancakes (sticking irritatingly to the pan), stir soup, and scrape slightly burned chicken wings from the tray onto the large Santa Claus platter. But it is all fine because, like Mom, I care deeply without caring at all. I look put together, our friends are devouring the curried coconut shrimp, the bubbly is cold and flowing, and "Festival of Carols" is exulting in the background. I mostly get it right.

It wasn't until a few days later when our friends shared some photos of the night that I realized the resemblance. Not so much physically, but in the expression of dogged persistence, the gene that had me hauling bags up to the Harlem Metro-North train station, the blood that had me on my feet all day single-handedly making this happen. The difference was, unlike with Mom, in the photos there are two other adults standing with me by the stove, helping to get the hot stuff out. My cheeks look flushed from the heat, my legs are sweating and itching against my tights. First Lady look-alike I am not. Still, I did it. And after the initial stress, I was able to enjoy my own party.

Becoming a woman is a process that has been revealed to me in stages. I can fold a fitted sheet by myself and make sure to get enough fiber in my diet, but there are still days I shy from the difficult realities of adulthood. Pulling off the family's Christmas tradition without my mom made me feel like an adult. I glimpsed what it meant to be the matriarch, the keeper of traditions. There is a moment when children understand their parents. *This is what she did all those years. That is how he kept us all together.* The invisible role becomes plain. Looking at those photos, I was seeing what it meant to be the mother. I was twenty-nine, digging in my heels against thirty. My aunts and uncles were asking when I was going to have a baby. There were days when I asked that myself, but I was still wondering most days if I was ready to be an adult. Surveying the people I had brought together around that kitchen island, though, I began to think that perhaps I was.

Curried Coconut Shrimp with Sweet-and-Sour Dipping Sauce

MAKES ABOUT 3 DOZEN

Our Christmas hors d'oeuvres may change from year to year, but Coconut Shrimp (and crab cakes) are *always* on the menu.

2 cups all-purpose flour, divided

2 tablespoons curry powder, divided

1 tablespoon sugar

1/2 teaspoon salt

8 ounces unsweetened shredded coconut

2 pounds (16 to 20 count) shrimp, peeled but tails intact, preferably wild

1 cup pepper jelly

1/4 cup rice wine vinegar

1/4 cup chopped fresh cilantro

6 cups peanut oil or vegetable oil

Measure 1 cup flour into medium bowl. Whisk remaining cup of flour with 2 teaspoons of curry powder, sugar, salt, and 1 cup of water in another bowl to form a smooth, thin batter. Measure coconut and remaining 4 teaspoons of curry powder in a third bowl.

Working one at a time, dredge shrimp in flour, shaking off excess. Holding shrimp by the tail, dip it in batter, allowing excess to drip off. (Thin batter with extra water as it thickens during this process.)

Having made a well in the coconut, drop in batter-coated shrimp; cover it with coconut, pressing so that it adheres. Lay shrimp on a large wire rack; repeat with remaining shrimp. Freeze for at least 30 minutes before frying. (Can be covered and frozen for several weeks.)

Make the sauce by heating jelly, vinegar, and cilantro in a small saucepan; set aside.

Heat oven to 200°F. Heat oil in an 8-quart soup kettle to 350°F. Set a wire rack over a baking sheet. Fry the shrimp in batches, making sure not to overcrowd the pan and turning each shrimp halfway through, until golden, 2 to 3 minutes. Transfer to wire rack and keep warm in the oven while frying remaining shrimp. Serve with sauce alongside.

18.

Forty Pounds Lighter,
Ten Years Later

pam

TEN YEARS AGO I LOST FORTY POUNDS. I'M NOT A TWELVE Stepper, but I know my inner addict, and food and drink have always been my vice. It took me nearly four decades to figure out there was no point in dieting. Unless you got honest about why you ate more than your body was really needing or asking for, you would never achieve lasting health. Still, my dark side emerges when one of two things happens. I work too hard and don't take time for the daily rituals that sustain my total well-being. Or, I become the "savior," taking care of everybody except myself.

To paraphrase Robert Frost, "I have had a lover's quarrel with food." I couldn't help but pass on some of that quarrel to my daughters, who also love food and struggle with it. And I am only bequeathing what I inherited.

My mother was one of five Ivey sisters, all curvy and known for their plump rumps—"Ivey hips" we called them.

When all the sisters got together and visited around the kitchen table, I listened as they gossiped and told new versions of the old family stories. Mostly, it all came back to food—how long they cooked their grits, how much they paid for coffee, their new method for frying chicken, where to get good pecans, which store had the best sausage, what brand of mayonnaise they preferred. Maybe it's because I only remember our big holiday meals, but it seemed the superabundant feasts and the obsession with food was their emphatic insistence that the hard times of the Great Depression were over.

From a physically active farming family, Dad was trim until shortly before I was born. He was out of work for several months and blamed his weight gain on sitting around. He may have got his paunch from sitting on the couch, but I believe he traded his alcohol addiction for a sweet tooth, and that's where he got his potbelly. For that lifesaving trade my mother is grateful and so am I.

It wasn't just that food was important in the larger clan. Food was a big deal for our little nuclear family, too. Nearly every Sunday after church, Dad grilled something—his lemon chicken, ribs, or steaks. And Mom baked regularly. There was always a hunk of chocolate or coconut cake hanging around or a slice of meringue pie to be had. She made candy, too—divinity, fudge, peanut brittle, Martha Washington balls, and more.

The neighbors started circling just as Mom and Dad churned canisters of homemade banana ice cream or started peeling peaches from a big basket they had just bought. A day of fishing or scalloping almost always climaxed with a big fry. And in winter, friends would gather as Dad pulled a big burlap sack of Apalachicola oysters out of the trunk. Some got shucked, others grill-roasted, the rest Mom turned into stew.

All the time we spent in church, you'd think God was the priority. Southern churches have big eating traditions, and beneath all our God-talk I think our faith was really invested in the surpassing ecstasy of a great meal—at church or with just the three of us. Only after I married did I realize Mom served dessert at lunch and dinner, and usually something sweet in between. Open up—it's the sweet manna of heaven. Glory be!

I am grateful for my food heritage, but the quarrel started early. When I was eight years old, Mom put me on my first diet. She got the doctor to prescribe diet pills and started measuring out my food. For a time I remember writing down everything I ate in a little notebook and calculating the calories. I was not to exceed one thousand a day.

Readying Mom and Dad's house for sale a few years ago, I found a cache of childhood photos—birth through college graduation—and noticed the yo-yo weight pattern even back then. I was normal at six, a little chubby at eight, okay at ten, definitely ballooning in junior high, downright thin in early high school, not bad at graduation. In college I was as thin as I'd ever be. One of the perks of attending a dry university: I never gained the freshman fifteen. When I got married, the serious life of feast and famine began.

Since David and I both grew up in fundamentalist Christian families and communities, getting married was our emancipation. In the first few years of marriage we made up for lost time, and food was a big part of our pleasure and discovery. We ate out a lot. I cooked a lot. There were spur-of-the-moment drinks and impromptu trips to the local pie shop. Watching late-night TV with a midnight snack was almost ritual. I splurged at work, too. My standard lunch out with colleagues was a patty melt and fries.

My fifteen came the freshman year of my marriage. To shed it I followed my brother-in-law's diet plan, drinking only liquids until the scale hit 120. I celebrated with a half bag of Doritos. And so it went for the next twenty-five years—work, reward, diet, burden, binge, purge. I lost big time on the Scarsdale Diet, the Rotation Diet, the Cabbage Soup Diet, the Heart Surgery Prep Diet, low-fat, high-protein, diet shakes and supplements, only to gain it all back within months. Once I got into the food business it was easy to blame my girth on work ("I have to eat, it's part of the job"), stubbornly blind to so many of my fit colleagues.

I had grown up in a rich and colorful culture where food was revered and indulged, but the system didn't teach me when and how much of it to eat. The guiding principle behind my Depression-scarred family was eat, drink, and be merry, for tomorrow we could all go hungry. If not, there's always a diet.

I passed on to my daughters that same sense of eat now, worry tomorrow. It wasn't until they left home, and I was alone, that I finally figured out how much to eat and when.

In 2003 our nest emptied, dramatically. Maggy was heading off to England for a junior year abroad and Sharon was starting her freshman year of college in Massachusetts. But I wasn't sitting mournfully in the kids' vacant bedrooms, because David and I were also moving. After eleven years in New Hope, Pennsylvania, we were heading back to Connecticut where David had been an assistant right out of seminary.

A dramatic move, both girls gone, and a husband caught up in the thrill of an exciting new job. It all happened at once. Alone and in a new community I was disoriented, physically exhausted, emotionally spent, and the heaviest I had ever been. Close to two hundred pounds, I was bitter at all the sacrifices I had made to raise the girls and get them into great schools, all I had done to enhance David's life and work, and no one was the least bit grateful. I had ceased to be useful, and everyone had thoughtlessly moved on. My family didn't give a damn about me.

In a new community—a minister's wife to boot—I had no one to talk to. Who in the parish wanted to hear that the new rector and his wife weren't in sync? I had a choice. I could slink away or I could try to dig my way out. The pull to go into hiding was strong. After all, the hands-on parenting phase was over, and the girls were more or less launched. Why not return to New Hope in enchanting Bucks County where I was comfortable, rent a little cottage, and live among friends who appreciated my gift of hospitality and bawdy sense of humor and wouldn't judge my heft?

And when it came to my extra pounds, David, who still fit into his jeans from high school, couldn't understand why I was incapable of losing weight. His pat response was always "just exercise a little more and eat a little less." Simple for him in theory, but not for me in execution.

That first year in Darien, David and I would go on long

walks. There was silence, more silence, then talk of our unhappiness. I would lay out my catalogue of complaints: all that I had done for him and our family. How I had contributed way more than my share to the family budget and generously hosted church parties, which brought me pleasure, but mostly benefited him. I planned our vacations, paid bills, did laundry, grocery shopped, got three great meals on the table every day. In short, I was a good wife *and* a good husband. So I had this one little flaw. Why couldn't he overlook that in view of everything else I did, God dammit?

This was the second time in our marriage we had fallen out of love. I remember our wondering aloud, "If we were to meet now, would we still be attracted to each other?" Sadly, the answer was, "Probably not." In my broken state I could not see that I needed to stop pleasing everyone at the price of my own neglect. I needed to trust that I was worthy of love simply for who I was, not for what I did. I wasn't there yet.

Short on women friends, I started seeing a therapist who helped me get my groove back. Whether or not it was true, Mary helped me believe I was strong and gifted, and that there were plenty of men who would find me attractive just as I was. My new doctor steered me to an acupuncturist who helped get my ailing body to heal. That time of physical and emotional healing strengthened me enough that my survivor side kicked in. Slowly, steadily I started to dig myself out.

I had yet to lose a pound, but as part of the healing process I also went to see a dermatologist. A Florida girl who spent many a summer in the sun, I was long overdue for a skin check. As part of the examination I had to put on hairnet-style underwear and bra and step into a dark box where someone took a series of photos, after which I was sent to an exam room for the results. The dermatologist walked into the room and said my skin was fine, but I seriously needed to lose weight. I was pissed. What right did a skin doc have commenting on my heft? I was outraged. Yet that insult was just what pushed me over the edge—into weight loss.

People often remark that shedding so much weight must have been difficult. Quite the opposite. The slow, steady weight gain, the accompanying mental anguish, and the resulting depression that comes from getting stuck was far more painful. Once I had done the hard work of emotional and physical healing, I was lighter in spirit, and in my strengthened state I started to care about myself. In turn, my invigorated body and mind seemed to know what it needed, and I just naturally started eating less . . . and getting off my duff. The result—with the help of vigorous exercise—was slow, steady weight loss over the course of eight months. I still smile every time I pick up a Costco-size box of kitty litter and remember what forty pounds feels like.

Exercise is the other half of the diet-exercise combo, but I had never been a natural athlete. There was no beloved youthful sport to reclaim. Instead I took to running, and running took to me. I gave it the only two gifts I had: diligence and determination. In return, running helped me learn to take care of myself.

Before I started the daily practice of running, I couldn't seem to avoid getting sucked into other people's stuff. *Make*

*my dinner, do my art project, mend my shirt, solve my prob-
lem.* The girls may have been in college, but they still found
ways to suck me in. Running gave me an out, literally—out
the door. When it was time to go for my run, I went. Even if
someone "needed me" just then. I wasn't headed for a bar
and girls' night out, I wasn't going to a spa for cucumbers on
my eyes, so who could argue with some good healthy exercise? Well, actually, plenty of people could and did. As much
as the family system didn't like my overweight state, it also
didn't like my absence. It had an addiction, too: me! At first
I got grief. There were complaints, questions, minor tan-
trums. "What's up with you?" Even well-meaning friends
asked earnestly if I wasn't taking this running thing a bit
too far. Eventually they started to see that my taking care of
myself didn't mean I wasn't available. I was legitimately
caring for myself, which meant I could legitimately care for
them. Counterintuitively, my caring less resulted in their
caring more for themselves, and for me.

Running played to my strengths, but it also worked because I rarely had an excuse not to do it. I didn't need a gym
and needed no special equipment. Weather conditions didn't
have to be just right. As long as I donned the right attire it
could be frigid or sweltering, and I could still get in my run.
Traveling? What better way to see a new city than head out
for a trot? I started with a couple of miles and then bumped
it up to four. Then I ran a six-mile race, which inspired one
marathon, and then nine more.

Running was not only good for me physically and emotionally, it was also empowering. I knew how to be badass in
the kitchen. Work twelve hours straight with a couple of

smoke breaks and a snack on the fly. Pick up a hot pan without flinching. Bandage a bloody finger and keep chopping. That kind of behavior built character, but it also took its pound of flesh by giving it back fortyfold.

Being tough on the running trail was different. Whereas the kitchen demanded I spend myself, a 26.2-mile race demanded I take care of myself. You will not make it on an excruciatingly long run if you don't properly feed and water your body before, during, and after. You must protect your body from the elements—sun, rain, heat, cold, wind—and guard against blistering, chafing, bleeding, and cramping. You must be willing, if necessary, to rise before dawn and go twenty miles in the dark before most people have taken their first sip of coffee, and you must live so that you are vibrant and ready to run at that early hour (which means you have to go to bed). This deep self-care was just the antidote to counter all of the years of self-neglect.

Pushing my limits in the kitchen had always made me feel strong, but nailing it on the running trail made me powerful. Eventually David's and my relationship recovered its equilibrium. I was looking good, feeling alive, and he was chasing me! Instead of my nagging him to come home and whining that we weren't spending enough time together, I became his priority. Now when he was still at the office, it was OK, because I knew he'd rather be with me.

There is a fine line between refusing to accept your partner—wrinkles, rolls, sags, and all—and pushing that person to live her best life. As angry as I was at the time that he would not accept me in my broken state, I credit David for pushing back when I wasn't willing to see the truth. In the end I was grateful he did not leave me or let me off the hook. Over the years I've done the same for him. It's what a good spouse does.

It's been ten years since I embraced my whole self, and what emerged from that time was a pleasurable way of eating—six little ritual meals—that I've adhered to ever since. Early morning herbal tea and seasonal fruit energizes until my interesting and ever-changing midmorning breakfast, which satisfies until a soup or salad lunch that keeps me content until afternoon tea and a sweet treat, which calms me until early evening wine and nibble, which helps me not to pick, so that I'm satisfied with a light supper.

Have I kept off every last pound? Not really. The fact is, life's not that tidy. When I lost the weight I didn't get a new brain. I still play badass in the kitchen, but now I take my ritual tea breaks and stop for a glass of wine and a good dinner. I still run, but I'm always fighting bum ankles and creaky knees. I continue to shoulder others' stresses and burdens, so it's only natural that I fall off the wagon. At least now I'm self-aware enough to know my trigger points and how to self-correct.

True confession. I've put back ten of the forty, but for someone like me, for whom food is a very real vice, I consider that a triumph. Without all that work a decade ago, getting at the heart of what makes me overeat and establishing my eating rituals, I would have gained it all back and more. For my sake and for my daughters, I wish I had figured it out sooner, but we always imagine that the best model we can give our children is perfection, when in fact, the most powerful gift is honesty.

Banana-Oat Muffins

MAKES 12 MUFFINS

Here's the kind of sweet treat I enjoy nearly every day with my afternoon cup of tea. A little something sweet like this keeps me from really overindulging. Like just the other day when someone gave me a big tin of M&M's and jelly beans. That first handful is so tempting, and then once in, it's nearly impossible to stop. Instead I reached for one of my approved treats, and that was it—the tin had lost its lure.

1 3/4 cups all-purpose flour

1 cup rolled oats

1/2 cup dark brown sugar

1 1/2 teaspoons baking powder

1/2 teaspoon baking soda

1/2 teaspoon salt

1 teaspoon cinnamon

1/2 teaspoon ground nutmeg

1/8 teaspoon allspice

1/8 teaspoon ground cloves

2/3 cup toasted pecans, chopped

2/3 cup dried cranberries (or raisins)

1 1/2 cups very ripe banana, pureed

1 cup plain (not Greek) yogurt

2 large eggs

1/4 cup milk

continued on next page

3 tablespoons vegetable oil

1 teaspoon vanilla extract

Heat the oven to 375°F, and move the oven rack to the middle position. In a medium bowl, combine the flour, oats, brown sugar, baking powder, baking soda, and salt. Add spices and stir to incorporate, then add the pecans and dried cranberries and stir again.

In a large bowl, whisk together the banana puree, yogurt, eggs, milk, oil, and vanilla. Pour dry ingredients into the wet ingredients and stir until just incorporated. Divide the batter evenly into a 12-cup muffin tin coated with nonstick cooking spray. Bake until golden brown, 25 to 30 minutes.

Allow muffins to cool for 5 minutes before removing them from the tins. Enjoy warm, or allow to cool completely and store in an airtight container for up to a week.

19.

Thighs That Bind

sharon

SOMETIMES I WONDER WHAT LIFE WOULD BE LIKE IF MY inner thighs didn't touch.

I could wear a dress on a hot summer day without having to worry that too much walking might lead to dreaded inner thigh chafing. I'd be able to hang on to a pair of jeans for more than a year because the inner seam wouldn't yield to unrelenting friction. I could wear real shorts (long ones don't count!) without having to yank them down every few steps.

I am certain that these benefits—and legions more—are delightful, but I have come to accept that this will never be my life. I have decades of experience and photographic evidence cataloguing the deep and abiding friendship that exists between my thighs. No matter how many miles I run, how many lunges I complete, how much kale I shovel down my gullet, my thighs will not be separated. They are in this together.

My story is unremarkable, particularly for a girl born in the mid-1980s. I ran around wild and free as a child, picking berries, climbing trees, playing tag. I was aware of my body—it worked fine, allowed me to move and play. It wasn't until middle school that I realized there was something deeply wrong: I wasn't skinny.

I struggled throughout high school and college to find ways to mold my curvy, athletic figure into the lithe, jiggle-free perfection I saw in movies, magazines, and the occasional real, live human. I had varying success, but never found a way to achieve that unrealistic goal in a sustainable way. The closest I've ever gotten to the hallowed inner thigh gap—and it wasn't *that* close—involved months of stress, Diet Coke, cigarettes, and the occasional package of ramen. This is not a lifestyle I recommend.

These days, I've come to terms with the state and fate of my thighs, in part because I know it's damn near impossible to swim out of your gene pool. When I look at my mom's body, I see myself. She is a little shorter, her hair is darker, and her skin tells the tale of a life well lived—scattered freckles from blissful days in the Florida sun, proud scars from decades in the kitchen, silvery stretch marks from bringing two girls into being—but what lies beneath our skin is almost identical. The same round face and upturned nose, the same gentle curve of the waist and wide flare of the hips, the same strong, sturdy legs.

I love my mother's body, and I love that I am built on her blueprint. I love that our genetic connection runs even deeper that our bones. We have the same iron will, back-breaking work ethic, and coarse sense of humor. Perhaps most important, though, we share the same fierce love of food. Some might claim nurture over nature on this one, arguing that I got swept up in the powerful and passionate current of my mother's tasting, creating, and serving. They would be right, but my profound reverence and respect for food runs deeper than that. Most of the time it feels twisted into the double helix of my DNA.

I know that between the genetics of soft curvature and an inherent love of food, there is little hope that my thighs will someday breeze past each other unscathed. I am mostly okay with that. When my mom was losing weight nearly a decade ago, someone gave her a little embroidered pillow that read, "Nothing tastes as good as being thin feels." While I appreciate the sentiment, I would respectfully like to call bullshit on that. I don't ever intend to live a life marked by wantonly stuffing my face with anything and everything, but I refuse to avoid truly amazing food—that perfect croissant, that earthy Bolognese, or that second (or third) glass of rare wine—in pursuit of being thin. The little aphorism fails to recognize that food is not only about taste; it's about experience and relationships.

There is plenty of research that says we should only take a dozen or so bites of our food and be done with it. They say that after the first few mouthfuls, the novelty wears off and we actually *taste* our food less. I've read the science, but I don't buy it. That may happen with some dishes, but in my experience, good food reveals itself in new ways over the course of the meal. Tomato sauce tastes purely tangy at first, but then the butteriness of roasted tomatoes comes out, followed by the richness of the cream and the fruitiness of the olive oil. I have a sip of wine, and then revisit the dish. This time, I am aware of how it feels in my mouth. I sink into the toothsome goodness of pasta and appreciate the way the sauce clings to it. As I eat, I am drawn into conversation with my husband, friend, or even a stranger—whomever I happen to be dining with—and our words get incorporated into our food, and both are bound up in the experience of being together, in the memory of that moment.

When I eat slowly and intentionally, food and relationships open up like a wine, revealing new aspects of themselves with each new bite and each passing moment. Not all meals taste as good as being thin feels, true. But some do.

For me the decision is relatively simple. When I look back on my life, I don't want to think, "Awesome. I managed to avoid butter, sugar, wine, cheese, and pasta, and I was thin my whole life. Sure, I usually passed on the food and wine that others enjoyed together, but I always fit into my high school jeans!" Instead, I want to remember the morning a friend made biscuits so light and tender I thought I might cry, the times Granny cooked us chicken and dumplings even though she didn't like them, the birthday night my husband (who *does not* bake) surprised me with a homemade coconut cake, the afternoon Maggy and I made paninis stuffed with tomatoes, bacon, and pesto and walked through Central Park, or the Thanksgiving our family polished off an enormous bottle of Pinot Noir in a rented condo in Atlanta.

I will eat—and love—quinoa and lentils, and I will revel in the abundance of fresh fruits and vegetables. But I refuse to eat only these things. In order to stay healthy and strong, I will run, swim, bike, walk, dance, hike, and do yoga— activities made possible by a life of good eating—but I will not torture myself to achieve a body I cannot sustain.

Of course, if I told you that I have completely accepted my body as it is, I would be lying. I haven't. On my best days, I feel comfortable and beautiful in my own flesh, but I also have days where I make grand plans for my bodily perfection. On those days I look wistfully at other women, wishing I had the genetics, the drive, or the self-discipline to dial my upper arm chub down to zero, to chisel my abs into long, lean lines, or to sculpt my butt into a perfect peach.

On both days, good and bad, I usually wind up in the kitchen making dinner. My husband is probably there as well, and there is some Spanish guitar or classic jazz lilting through our apartment. When I sidle up to the stove, Anthony probably nuzzles my neck while handing me a glass of wine or holds out a spoonful of his famous risotto for me to sample, and I think: *This* is what life is all about. I wouldn't trade it for the sleekest thighs in the world.

To me, there is something deeply liberating in knowing that no one—my husband included—loves me because my body is perfect. (Because even if it were now, it certainly wouldn't be forever.) Being imperfect gives me permission to live my life with great joy, a healthy dose of moderation, and a little excess, and it makes it okay for the years to manifest themselves on my body in marks, scars, and curves. I've seen what that looks like on my mother, and let me tell you, it's gorgeous.

Perhaps it's time to embroider that pillow with something like, "If you can't see daylight between your thighs, you might just be living right." Or maybe it's time to throw the old one out.

The Best Mushroom Risotto

SERVES 6 TO 8

This recipe is based on Anthony's father's tried-and-true method, and it is truly spectacular. One spoonful of this risotto compels me to remember that life *is* good—no matter what my thighs look like. Plus, I like to think that all of the constant stirring builds muscle and burns calories! I like to use a combination of fresh mushrooms, such as shiitakes, creminis, and portabellos, but you can use whatever you like. If you don't like mushrooms, just leave them out and increase the amount of chicken stock to 8 cups. I recommend using homemade chicken stock because it tends to be less salty and chicken-y than the store-bought stuff. If you don't have time to make your own, be sure to cut back on the salt in this recipe or dilute your stock with some water.

1 cup dried mushrooms

Extra-virgin olive oil

1 pound fresh mushrooms, cleaned and sliced

1/2 teaspoon dried thyme leaves

1/4 teaspoon crushed red pepper flakes

1 large onion, cut into small dice

Kosher salt and pepper

2 large garlic cloves, minced

2 cups Arborio rice

1 cup dry white wine

continued on next page

6 cups low-sodium chicken stock,
  preferably homemade

1 large pinch of saffron, optional

1 cup grated Parmigiano-Reggiano

2 tablespoons unsalted butter

Place the dried mushrooms into a heatproof bowl, pour 2 cups of boiling water over them, and cover with a plate. Allow the mushrooms to soak until they are tender and fully rehydrated, at least 30 minutes. When tender, remove the mushrooms from their soaking liquid and chop them finely. Be sure to save the soaking liquid (there should be about 1½ cups), as you will need it for cooking the risotto.

Heat a few teaspoons of olive oil in a large Dutch oven or heavy-bottomed pot over medium-high heat. When the oil is hot, place enough sliced fresh mushrooms in the pot to cover the bottom without crowding. Sprinkle the mushrooms with a little thyme, red pepper flakes, salt, and pepper, and sauté, stirring occasionally, until golden brown. Remove the cooked mushrooms from the pot, place them into a bowl, and set aside. Drizzle a little more olive oil into the pot, and repeat this process once or twice more until all the fresh mushrooms are browned and seasoned.

When all the mushrooms have been sautéed, reduce the heat under the pot to medium and heat 2 tablespoons of olive oil. Add the onions, 1 teaspoon of kosher salt, and a few grinds of black pepper; cook, stirring occasionally, until the onions are tender and translucent, 10 to 15 minutes. Add the garlic and cook until fragrant, about another minute. Increase the heat to medium-high; add the rice and cook, stirring frequently, until it starts to become translucent, 2 to 3 minutes. Add the wine and cook until it reduces almost completely, another 2 to 3 minutes.

Meanwhile, bring the chicken stock and saffron (if using) to a simmer in a medium saucepan. Reduce the heat to low and keep warm.

Add the mushroom soaking liquid to the rice and cook, stirring constantly, until the liquid has almost completely absorbed. Then add 1 ladleful of hot chicken stock and continue to cook, stirring constantly, until it is absorbed as well. Repeat this process until half the stock is gone. Add the chopped rehydrated mushrooms, stir to combine, and then continue to ladle hot stock into the risotto, stirring constantly and letting the rice absorb the stock completely before adding more, until all the stock has been used.

Taste the rice; it should be soft but toothsome. If it is done, add the sautéed mushrooms and stir to combine. If the rice needs more cooking, heat some water in the saucepan and continue cooking the rice, adding ladles of water and stirring frequently, until the rice is done. Then add the sautéed mushrooms.

When the rice is done and the mushrooms have been incorporated, turn off the heat, add the Parmigiano and butter, and stir until melted and incorporated. Season to taste with salt and pepper, if necessary, and serve immediately.

70.

Live to Eat

maggy

THERE WERE MANY SIGNALS THAT GRANNY AND PAPA WERE starting to decline. There were Granny's cancer diagnosis, Papa's cane and, ultimately, the walker. There were signs of dementia and the onset of listlessness and depression. Despite all these challenges, though, they could—and did—persevere and go on with life. But I knew for certain we were losing my beloved Granny and Papa when they both abruptly lost interest in food.

When they moved from their home of thirty-five years into a retirement community a few miles away, Mom, Dad, and I went to Panama City, Florida, to help them to sift through the last of their heirlooms and knickknacks. Travel-weary, we arrived late and hungry. In the glory years, we would have pulled into 8035 Highpoint Road to a feast of Southern comfort foods: Papa's famous lemon chicken or barbecued ribs, corn on the cob, grilled garlic bread, Le Sueur peas, and iceberg lettuce salad. A homemade cake enshrined in plastic on the counter, Sharon and I staring at it longingly throughout supper.

But Granny and Papa had long since stopped cooking. Their new apartment barely had a kitchen, and in all her crazed trips down to support them, Mom had found a new joint called Cato's Seafood Market and Steam Bar just off U.S. 231 that served fresh Gulf seafood, steamed to order. Formerly a 7-Eleven, Cato's wasn't an upmarket establishment. Bare tables were flanked by picnic benches and topped with plastic baskets holding paper towels, straws, a selection of hot sauces, and packets of saltine crackers.

It was strange to be sitting in a restaurant with Granny and Papa. In my lifetime we'd been to restaurants with them only a handful of times. Aside from buying us a Frosty at Wendy's on the way home from church or a road-trip lunch stop at Cracker Barrel, Granny and Papa didn't like to eat out. They knew they could make food better than whatever we'd be served at a restaurant and, more to the point, they were loath to spend the money. But we were in a new era.

Without hesitation, Mom, Dad, and I ordered the special: steamed Gulf shrimp, corn on the cob, and the house's version of Grecian potatoes. Granny, whose taste buds had been annihilated by round after round of chemotherapy, said she didn't want anything. Mom told her she had to eat something, but it was like haggling with a child. Finally, Granny ironically agreed to the "tiniest, tiniest child's portion." When the waitress came to take our order, Granny told the woman four times how she had no appetite, how small she wanted her portion to be, holding her hands two inches apart. It was all a little awkward. Mom had to explain to the poor server that the loss of appetite and taste was due to chemotherapy. "I'm so sorry, ma'am," she said to Granny.

Next Mom turned to Papa. "Dad, what do you want? Do you want the special?" As always in those final years, he seemed initially confused. He wasn't hungry, didn't want to eat. Papa was diabetic—Mom knew he really needed to eat. I'd come to accept Granny's waning interest in food as one more sadness of cancer and chemo. But was this all about the $14.99 price tag on the shrimp platter special? With the expense of the move, were they feeling even more anxious about money?

The server, radiating warmth, sensed the anxiety and mercifully intervened. "Not to worry," she said. "I know just what to bring y'all." Ten minutes later, one giant platter arrived with corn around the perimeter, the center piled high with boiled shrimp on one side and the Grecian potatoes on the other, lemon wedges scattered over the plate. With no individual platters, no one had to eat more than they wanted, nor could anyone really calculate the cost. Granny and Papa picked while we gorged. I ate because I was hungry, but seeing my papa, who in his time could inhale a rack of ribs (and pronounce it a snack), picking awkwardly at one or two shrimp that Mom had to peel for him made my heart sick. I knew we were staring down the end. My grandparents, who had been the embodiment of "live to eat," were refusing food. It wasn't about money; they'd just lost their appetite.

There was a lot about my grandparents that we did not emulate, like their particular religious beliefs or conservative social values, but as a family we took their live-to-eat philosophy and ran with it, ultimately making it our own.

Granny and Papa believed passionately that the meals they made were far better (and cheaper) than anything they could get at a restaurant. To that belief, we added our lusty *Amen*. As a family, one of our favorite mealtime games is to pose the question, "How much would you pay for this at a restaurant?" Then we all guess—the more outlandish the price the better. "How much for these buttery, beautiful scallops? Thirteen dollars a plate! Times four? That's fifty-two dollars right there!" and "What kind of a markup on this fine wine we got for eleven dollars? It would be at least forty dollars in a restaurant."

We also got Granny and Papa's love/hate relationship with the scale, which in their home had pride of place not in their bathroom, but next to their kitchen table. With the exception of Dad, we all took on this strange ambivalence.

With a petite 4' 10" frame, Granny was always fretting her heft, ever conscious not only of her own weight but that of others. The mere mention of a family member or church friend would draw the Granny-ism "Oooh, she gained" if the person had put on a few pounds. And if Mom, Sharon, or I came to visit a little trimmer than usual it was, "Oooh, you look like you lost." She was so fixated on weight, hers and ours, but she could never stop feeding us, literally pushing food from her plate onto ours with the back of her fork. And since Granny had no patience for leftovers crowding her fridge, many a meal was ruined by her insistence that each basket, bowl, or platter be licked clean (which was absurd as they always cooked for a crowd twice the size).

Seemingly gigantic at six feet tall, Papa had slender, al-most delicate arms and legs attached to his signature potbelly, which was not soft or fatty, but perfectly rotund and curiously hard. Sharon and I loved to poke his paunch. That belly was a colossal weak spot for retaliation against his tickling, and a natural pillow when we grew tired. I remember one autumn Mom mentioned to us in passing that Papa had lost some weight. For her this was great news, but Sharon and I, just kids at the time, both started to cry. "But we don't want him to lose his Papa-belly!" we said. We were nervous to see what this new, trimmer papa looked like, but when he arrived a few weeks later for Christmas, we were relieved to see that it was mostly still there.

Every summer Granny and Papa got us for two weeks—no parents. It was grand time: they at parenting, we at being children. They used to joke that when they were with us they got to be teenyboppers. The highlight of their typical day might be a trip to the Winn-Dixie, but when the grands came they went all out. There were trips to St. Andrew's State Park and the beach, mornings of fishing off the dock, and afternoons spent making "dirt dessert." But there was no activity more eagerly anticipated than a trip to Panama City Beach's water park, Shipwreck Island. After a night of fitful sleep in anticipation, we'd lather up with sunscreen and head out for a day of rides, slides, and wave pools. While our grandparents' favorite attraction was the Lazy River, they still managed to sit on the spongy, rubber mats and fly down the Zoom Flume right behind us.

If these parks make most of their money on eight-dollar hot dogs and a watery Coke for three bucks, they lost money on us. This family never spent a dime beyond the price of admission. Before heading out in the morning, Granny and

Papa would pack a cooler with tuna and egg salad sandwiches on fluffy white bread, dill pickles, sour cream and onion and barbecue potato chips, homemade cookies, leftover slices of coconut cake, and cans of Coke wrapped in wet paper towels and tin foil to keep them extra-cold. Come 1 P.M. we'd have our hands stamped and exit the park, Granny, Sharon, and I making a beeline for the picnicking area to claim a table while Papa went to retrieve the cooler. After hours of nonstop frolic in the hot Florida sun, we devoured lunch like a hungry herd of piglets. We were young, but Sharon and I knew that picnic filled us like no boiled and limp amusement park hot dog ever could. And Granny and Papa knew it was a fraction of the cost, too.

Their marriage was a traditional one, not only because they were a product of their time, but also because they were deeply observant Christians who lived out Ephesians 5:22–23, "Wives, submit to your husbands as to the Lord. For the husband is the head of the wife as Christ is the head of the church." Papa worked, Granny kept up the home. Papa made decisions, Granny agreed without question. But in retirement, their relationship evolved in one nontraditional way: They cooked together. And Papa almost always did the dishes. They were happiest in the kitchen together, feeding the people they loved, rotating through comfort classics like Frito pie, chicken tetrazzini, chicken and dumplings, and fresh fried fish and hush puppies. These meals were served with Southern side dishes: overcooked vegetables like yellow squash, collard greens, and Papa's famous corn bread. But Sharon and I looked forward to their desserts more than anything: homemade summer fruit pies, coconut or German chocolate cake, and our favorite—banana pudding. We used to joke with Granny that we preferred it when Papa cut our slices of cake. While her slices were paper thin, Papa cut off thick, generous slabs. "Della Ruth," he would crow proudly, "they ask *me* because I give them a slice of cake that has *two* sides!" We could always rely on Papa's own sweet tooth to defend our right to more cake.

After dinner there was nothing to do but park ourselves in front of the boob tube, watching the same classic movies from the good old days that Papa kept in his extensive VHS library: *High Society*, *White Christmas*, and our very favorite, *Margie*. When we got a little older, we added *The Bridge on the River Kwai*, *Doctor Zhivago*, and *Gone with the Wind* to the rotation. After exhausting those titles, we switched to reruns of *I Love Lucy*, *The Dick Van Dyke Show*, and *I Dream of Jeannie*. All the while Granny and Papa reclined in their La-Z Boys and laughed out loud at "that silly old Lucy" as they flossed their teeth free of the day's meals and Sharon and I sprawled out on our full bellies in front of them.

Our visits lasted so long that house and garden work could not be put off until after we'd gone home. Granny and Papa's large yard was a wild botanical beast they barely kept at bay, so every couple weeks the property needed to be cleared of limbs and small branches brought down by summer storms before it could be mowed. They were at an age where they should have been paying someone to do this kind of physical work for them, but this was yet another thing they couldn't spend money on.

When we weren't there, Granny and Papa simply collected all the debris and burned it in their fire pit, which was really just a hole in the ground down by the lake. Afterward, Granny hopped on the riding lawn mower and sheared a few inches off the thick, bristly St. Augustine grass. But when we were visiting, they made use of our youthful energy (read: free labor), enticing us to work with the promise of something fun at the end—a weenie roast. By grandparent magic they turned the just-shoot-me task of collecting sticks into something we approached like a sport. The more sticks we could gather, the better the fire would be. With the promised reward of hot dogs and s'mores, picking up sticks was a chore we relished.

At the end of our summer trip, Mom and Dad were always so happy to have us home. We were less enthusiastic about seeing them, reluctantly heading back home to the tedium of school and homework, simple weeknight suppers with no dessert, and very limited TV watching (definitely no cable). But Granny and Papa continued to show their love from afar. Between visits, they'd send cards for every holiday and small souvenirs from their travels and call every week. When we went to college, they sent care packages filled with grandparent-y things like packs of new socks, toothbrushes, and giant sleeves of gum. When I moved to England, they sent boxes that held the two things they knew I loved but couldn't find in my exile: bags of grits and cans of Le Sueur peas. Granny and Papa, who double-checked every grocery receipt for errors before leaving the store, thought nothing of spending $75 to ship such heavy items from Florida to England, because they were sending far more than grits and peas. They were sending love. That's what Southern food is.

Love cooked until it falls off the bone, melts in your mouth, runs down your chin, or drowns your heart in the oil of gladness.

But there was no greater gift than the one that arrived in old, dented tins and large plastic tubs when Granny and Papa came for Christmas each year. They spent the week prior to travel making what ultimately became their traditional Christmas confections: peanut brittle, fudge, rocky road, Cap'n Crunch candy, an assortment of decorated sugar cookies coated in thick white frosting, and church windows—multicolored mini marshmallows held together by chocolate, rolled into a log, and sliced to resemble stained glass. All this was packed into suitcases and carry-ons and unloaded in our living room before they'd even had a chance to get their luggage to the bedroom. My most sought-after cookie was the snowman shape. The story goes that when I was about five years old, Granny asked me over the phone what sweets I wanted them to bring. I shouted over the line, "*snowman* cookies!" and she made them every year thereafter. When age and distance prevented us from being together, Granny and Papa sent boxes filled with the treats they knew had become synonymous with Christmas. They loved knowing that they were needed, even when we grew up.

When people who live to eat lose their appetite, death has already picked the lock and is halfway in the back door. So there I sat on the picnic bench at Cato's Seafood Market and Steam Bar, staring mournfully at my pile of shells. With nothing much to do, Granny was cleaning her section of the table with a pad of napkins and Papa was accepting one more mouthful from a daughter trying to ward off insulin shock. It had come to this. The one thing we shared—despite all that separated these Baptist teetotalling Rebels from us liberal Yankee Episcopalians—the one thing that held us in thrall to one another, food, was gone. I wanted to cry.

I could see that my grandparents were slowly ebbing away, and that as a result, their legacy in Mom and Sharon and Dad and me was gone. I was a "live to eat" cook because Mom was and Granny and Papa were before her. It had been so carefree to carry on that tradition as the third generation. But now I could see a passing, and how soon it would be just Mom ahead of me. It seemed harder to carry the weight of the tradition handed down to me. I did not want to drop it. And I did not ever want to lose my appetite.

I want to be hungry till I'm gone.

Banana Pudding

SERVES 6

After all those years of loving my granny's banana pudding I finally got around to asking her for the recipe. Her response? "Oh, it's just the recipe on the side of the Nilla Wafers box!" This is a slightly more homemade version of the side-of-the-box classic.

1/2 cup sugar

2 tablespoons cornstarch

Pinch salt

2 large egg yolks

1 can (12 ounces) evaporated milk, plus 1/2 cup milk to equal 2 cups total

1 tablespoon vanilla extract, divided

1 cup heavy cream

48 vanilla wafers

3 bananas, peeled and sliced

Whisk the sugar, cornstarch, and salt in a medium saucepan. Just before adding milk, whisk in egg yolks, and then turn heat to medium and vigorously whisk in milk. Continue to whisk occasionally and then more frequently as it heats, until mixture boils and thickens to pudding consistency; remove from heat; stir in 2 teaspoons of the vanilla. Cover with a sheet of plastic wrap

continued on next page

pressed directly on the surface to keep a skin from forming; cool to room temperature.

When ready to assemble, whip the cream with remaining teaspoon of vanilla to soft peaks. Arrange 4 vanilla wafers in each of 6 wide goblets. Add a few banana slices to each goblet. Top with a generous 2 tablespoons each of pudding and whipped cream. Repeat, arranging 3 vanilla wafers in each goblet, along with a few more banana slices, and a couple of generous tablespoons each of remaining pudding and cream. Top with remaining vanilla wafer and garnish with a few banana slices. Cover and refrigerate until cookies soften, a couple of hours and up to overnight. Serve.

21

Raising the Bar

pam

AFTER THIRTY-SIX YEARS OF MARRIAGE, DAVID AND I FINALLY built a bar. It's not just a little dry cubby with booze in the bottom cabinet, glasses on the top. It's well endowed with an ice machine, sink, under-the-counter fridge, and wine cooler, all the gleaming stemware hanging from racks on the ceiling. A stunning slab of sinker cypress runs the length.

Someone years ago surveying my future might have predicted that such a taproom was either impossible or inevitable.

I was raised in the Bible Belt by a recovering alcoholic father and a mother who kept him in line, so alcoholism was a constant theme in our family.

One of my earliest memories—I must have been three— was eating cake at one of his AA meetings on the anniversary of his sobriety. The summer I turned five we moved to

Panama City, Florida, and an independent Baptist church became his new AA.

No longer did Dad did go off to meetings by himself. We all went to church. A lot. Sunday School and church in the morning, training union and church again on Sunday night. Back again for prayer meeting on Wednesday night, with revivals, missionary conferences, and other special events peppered in throughout the year.

Devout church attendance, along with frequent sermons condemning firewater, kept Dad straight. "Wine is a mocker, strong drink is raging and whosoever is deceived thereby is not wise" (Proverbs 20:1). Somehow they ignored the scores of Bible verses extolling the pleasures of wine and fixed obsessively on the few that warned of its potential dangers.

Mom reinforced the booze ban. Anytime the subject came up, she delivered the family line: "There's trouble in every bottle." She was so strict I wasn't even allowed to go to Lum's Restaurant in town because their hot dogs were steamed in beer.

I imagine losing friends was one of the most difficult things about my father (and mother) going dry. It's nearly impossible for an alcoholic to hang out with drinkers, and imbibers often feel guilty in the presence of principled abstainers. But blood was thicker than booze, and Mom and Dad found a way to stay connected with our relatives and a few of their friends from the drinking days. This inner circle of family and friends was very respectful of Dad's condition. They never drank in our home, and when we got together on their turf they usually asked permission and always kept it discreet.

Unlike Maggy and Sharon, I did not go to teenage sleepovers and get throw-up sick on peach schnapps. In fact, before I was twenty-one I had tasted alcohol only a couple of times. My cousin Patricia let me sip a little sherry at one of her bridge parties. When I was sixteen I went to Chicago with my piano teacher for a week of study. Hoping for a good time, the hotel bellboy delivered complimentary screwdrivers to my friend and me.

Three days after graduating from a religious college so strict that unchaperoned dating was not even permitted, David and I got married. Out for dinner one night on our honeymoon, the waiter asked for my drink order. I was a month shy of twenty-one, and the thought of ordering something besides iced tea had never occurred to me.

After that dry honeymoon, David and I moved hundreds of miles from the Florida Panhandle to Chicago. In our new freedom we began to enjoy the fruit of the vine—a glass of burgundy with our steak, a bottle of Lancer's or Mateus (this was, after all, the seventies) out for dinner. We started buying stemware and picking up cordial glasses at tag sales.

My parents' first visit, we hid everything—the gadgets, the glasses, the bottles—and packed them all in boxes in the attic. But I did not hide that we enjoyed drinking in moderation. I hoped for understanding. Instead I got chastising. Nothing good came from drinking. It was a slippery slope. What if I was like Dad?

Over the years I came to realize that drinking symbolized all they didn't like—my church (which serves up the real stuff at communion), my political leanings, my decorating, my lifestyle, my parenting, my accent (or loss thereof). I felt their rejection, and I was hurt. Now that I have two daughters who've left the nest and broken with some of our family traditions, I understand how my parents felt. They perceived I had abandoned all they had taught and modeled for me when, in fact, I was just becoming myself.

For the sake of our relationship we mostly avoided religious and political discussions when they visited, but at least we stopped hiding the bottles and glasses. It was all there, we just didn't touch it. No one spoke of it. This uneasy compromise went on for twenty years. But as someone for whom eating and drinking well are virtually inseparable, I eventually tired of dry holidays and cocktail-less vacations. I finally reasoned that since Dad had been sober for more than fifty years, my sipping a glass of Chablis in his presence was not about to bump him off the wagon.

Actually, it was more than that. David and I began to see how we had failed to grow up as adult children. The problem was not with "them" but with us. It was our responsibility to act like *adult* children and simply live our lives. In trying to honor them we had become infantilized, blaming them for what we couldn't do.

We finally made the move by enjoying wine with dinner—a glass each on the table, bottle out of sight. It was never easy. I always felt their silent disapproval. When Maggy and Sharon came of drinking age, I realized the strength of Mom and Dad's judgment. I understood my fear, but I was surprised at my kids'. Having spent weeks at a time with their grandparents during their formative years, they knew firsthand Mom and Dad's strong convictions. I was glad that I had already taken the risk and prepared the way, so they could drink reasonably and responsibly in front of their grandparents.

In spring of 2013 my dad was losing it mentally—and fast. Mom had been through four full rounds of chemotherapy in eight years and was suffering from depression and neuropathy. Her oncologist prescribed a little Percocet to ease the mental and physical pain. Finally she got a little relief. Even in his confused mental and verbal state, Dad made it clear he did not like Mom taking this pain pill. As much as the doctor tried to convince Dad that Mom needed the meds, he was concerned that she might share his weakness and get addicted.

Dad died on May 10, 2013, a few months after that doctor's appointment. Mom's birthday is June 22nd, and that year we needed a reason to celebrate. Maggy, Sharon, and Mom, along with my two cousins, Mom's only living sister, and I gathered for a few days at a condominium on Panama City Beach. My cousins brought a little vodka and tonic. I picked up some gin. During those days together, everyone but Mom enjoyed a little predinner cocktail overlooking the Gulf.

Even though Mom wasn't participating, all the anxiety about our drinking was gone. One night as she got up from the dinner table, I handed her the night meds, including her pain pill. She looked up at us all with a sheepish grin, and said, jokingly, "I'm hooooked!" Even though she could never allow herself to enjoy a cocktail, she realized her nightly pill accomplished the same purpose. She was no longer our judge.

That same trip to Florida coincided with the bar construction. Except for the bar top everything had been ordered. Attempts to match our five-year-old granite kitchen countertop were not successful. David had found something close and was about to place the order. But on a whim one night, I decided to stop at Grayton Beach Bar and Grill to see my friends Deb and Johnny Earles's new restaurant. As I walked through the door, my eye caught the gorgeous slab of wood that spanned the bar—deadhead or sinker cypress, they called it.

I gushed. I inquired. It turns out the mill was just down the road. The next morning I called the owner and told him what I needed. By the time I got there he had already picked out my piece, a stunning ten-foot long, two-and-a-half-inch-thick, three-hundred-pound beauty. The love was strong and immediate. I messaged a picture to David, but I wasn't looking for approval. I had already made up my mind.

The log had been submerged for nearly two hundred years, the man said, absorbing the water's distinct coloring.

"Where did my piece come from?" I asked.

"Near the Apalachicola River," he responded.

"My mom, dad, and I used to fish nearby at a place called Howard's Creek," I said.

He started to smile. "That's exactly where this piece came from."

The emotion was overwhelming. I choked up. Somehow I had found my way to a piece of wood from a log that had been pulled from the creek where my dad and I used to fish. Then I remember Dad and me sitting in his Boston Whaler. I hook my worm and throw it in. As soon as it hits the water, my cork starts to bob. I pull in a bream the size of Dad's hand. He's proud. I repeat the process and immediately catch another. "Looks like we've stumbled on a bed," Dad exclaims. He throws in his line, and we spend the next half hour catching one fish after another. We could look for another slough, but that'd be greedy. We've caught a cooler full of fish for tonight's fry.

That sinker cypress has transformed a lovely bar into a showpiece. That slab of wood conjures my father's spirit, and as I shake cocktails, uncork wine, and uncap beer, I love my dad. And as I sense his pride, I feel pleasure.

The Creole Sazerac

MAKES 1 DRINK

Sharon's husband, Anthony, is a Presbyterian minister. He's also a gifted cocktail maker. The Creole Sazerac, a riff on the New Orleans classic, is one of his creations that has become a signature Anderson family drink.

1 1/2 ounces aged dark rum

1/2 ounce rye whiskey

1/2 ounce simple syrup

1/4 teaspoon absinthe

3 dashes Peychaud's bitters

1 dash old-fashioned bitters

Lemon peel, for garnish

Combine the rum, rye, simple syrup, absinthe, and bitters in a mixing glass, add a handful of ice, and stir vigorously. Strain into a cocktail glass and serve with a lemon peel.

Simple Syrup

MAKES 1 CUP

The key to simple syrup is equal parts water and sugar. I usually make a large batch because it keeps indefinitely in the fridge.

1 cup sugar

1 cup water

Heat water and sugar in a saucepan over medium heat until the sugar dissolves. Allow to cool, transfer to a container, and refrigerate.

Union Square Café-Inspired Bar Nuts

MAKES 2 1/2 POUNDS OR 2 QUARTS

We've been making these nuts ever since the *Union Square Café Cookbook* came out in 1994, and we've roasted hundreds, if not thousands, of pounds of them. Over the years we've tried changing up the recipe, but it just doesn't get any better than this. If you don't shop at Costco, try to find bulk roasted salted nuts and create your own mix. You can halve the recipe and roast them in a 13 × 9-inch pan, but we eat them so regularly—and give them away, too—that it doesn't make sense to make them in smaller quantity.

> 1 Costco-size container (40 ounces or 2 1/2 pounds) premium roasted, salted mixed nuts
>
> 4 teaspoons butter
>
> 1/4 cup minced fresh rosemary
>
> 4 teaspoons packed dark brown sugar
>
> 1 teaspoon cayenne pepper
>
> 1 teaspoon kosher salt

Adjust oven rack to middle position and heat oven to 350°F. Spread nuts on a 18 × 12-inch rimmed baking sheet. Roast until fragrant and slightly darker in color, 10 to 12 minutes.

Meanwhile, microwave butter in a small bowl until melted; stir in rosemary, sugar, cayenne, and salt. Pour roasted nuts in a large bowl. Add rosemary mixture and use a rubber spatula to make sure herb paste completely coats the nuts. Pour nuts back onto the cookie sheet and cool. Serve warm or at room temperature. (Can be stored in an airtight container up to 1 month.)

22

The Mat Under
the Mango Tree

maggy

A T TWENTY-FIVE YEARS OLD I MADE THE DECISION TO GET out of domestic social work. Frankly, I got bored helping people—over the phone—navigate the bureaucratic regulations tangled around housing and unemployment benefits. The world needs social workers—they're angels. I was just wingless.

I set my sights instead on international development. I wanted to work with people who lived in a parallel universe, who had nothing and no one to fall back on. Before applying for a master's degree in the field, though, I thought it wise to get some real world experience.

Serendipitously, a friend of mine was able to connect me with a young woman who had just started a grassroots organization building primary schools in Malawi, Africa. We met and immediately hit it off. I thought I was joining the team just to raise awareness and some money in London. But in a matter of weeks she was asking if I would join her for a few months as she broke ground on her first school in a remote northern village called Chisala. I was elated, but how could I pull this off? Andy, ever supportive, saw the opportunity and agreed that I should take temporary leave from my job and go. He helped me pack, drove me to London Heathrow Airport, and, though he'd desperately miss me, sent me off with his love.

That is how I found myself working for three months on a school construction project in Malawi, the small country dubbed "The Warm Heart of Africa." That first trip was magical. I had heard that Africa was enchanting, majestic, enthralling. Once you had drunk deeply of this continent, people said, you could leave, but you'd never forget and forever yearn to return. That it exactly what happened to me.

It wasn't all enchantment, though. During my time there I often ate lunch with the nurses I had befriended at the village health clinic. They told me stories of women walking twenty miles to the nearest town—*while in labor*—and having to stop and give birth on the side of the road. Women and babies were dying of complications that could easily be addressed "... if only they had been with a doctor." The school we were building was much appreciated, but for these nurses, the most urgent need was a maternity clinic.

And so it was that, without any experience or means, I promised the people of Chisala that we would build a maternity clinic. I still don't know what moved me to make such a wild offer. But I said I would return with the funds for construction, if they would help by making all the bricks.

I returned to England and spent the next two years planning and fund-raising for the maternity clinic while buried in classes and course work for my full-time master's program in International Development. This was the fall of 2008, and I had no idea I'd be a first-time fund-raiser testing my skills during the worst financial crisis my generation had seen. From grant-writing and events to bake sales and charity runs, with nearly every ounce of free time we scraped together the $100,000 we needed just in time to break ground in August 2009. There were a few times when I thought I would have to accept that we might not be able to pull this off. I was embarrassed to find myself incapable and angry at the thought of disappointing my friends back in Chisala. The worry of potential failure burrowed into every crevice of my mind, but the demands of my master's program remained (to say nothing of my part-time job at our local pub). With the help of many, and sheer force of will, we reached our goal.

Just two weeks after I handed in my dissertation, Andy and I both quit our jobs (he wasn't going to miss this next adventure) and moved to Malawi to oversee the construction of the maternity clinic and doctor's house. When we got there in early August 2009 the community had been hard at work, hoping we would arrive, but not sure we'd actually keep our promise. There was almost no way to let them know that money had been raised, jobs had been quit, flights had been booked—we were unquestionably Malawi-bound. Nevertheless, on hope alone they kept up their end of the bargain: Hundreds of thousands of bricks had been made, the land for the clinic and doctor's house had been cleared and staked out, and most important, the committee to work with us had been elected by the villagers. These four men would help us to oversee the project and be our conduit to the people of Chisala. In the traditional structure of the village, this was key. If we were making mistakes they'd let us know; if we needed community support, they'd spread the word.

Like the first day of school in a room full of strangers, we could not have conceived how these four men would soon become our beloved partners. Matthews, a quiet older man with little to say, had cataract-glazed eyes and close-cut cotton white hair. Though one step behind physically and mentally, he was mild-mannered and kind. When he did speak up, his observations were always insightful. George, young and spry, had a wide smile exposing a set of impossibly large and perfect teeth, which mirrored his unfailingly positive outlook on absolutely *everything*. Then there was Chisiwawa, towering, scowling, and no-nonsense. He laughed exactly three times during our entire stay. He acted as our perennial naysayer and devil's advocate, an obnoxious but important role. And finally Elias, with his crooked and endless smile, was shrewd and focused—a most skilled problem solver and peacemaker. He led the charge with a personality that won over the Chisiwawas everywhere we went. Without him, we would have failed utterly. These four would labor alongside us and guide us; what we didn't know is that they would become our family.

From the start our days were filled with grueling physical labor. Go to town, load up the truck with sixty ninety-pound bags of cement, then drive the forty-five minutes back to Chisala. On the other end, the committee and construction crew would help us unload. "Good," the foreman would say, "we have cement. Now we are running out of bricks." And off we'd go, men, women, and children, to load the truck with bricks. We'd form a bucket brigade that within an hour would jam-pack the truck bed with four thousand bricks. Then we'd drive it, engine groaning, back to the construction site where the volunteers lined up to help us unload. Water for cement-making, quarry stone for foundations, timber for window frames. Loading and off-loading, that's how we spent 80 percent of our time. Any time and energy left over was spent contending with flooded roads, lengthy fuel shortages, and maddening government roadblocks and red tape.

At night, there was nothing to do but collapse. We lived for that first refreshing sip of Malawi gin and fizzy Schweppes tonic, freshly popped popcorn, and the BBC World Service. We cooked heaping portions of simple suppers made from local ingredients. We played cards, read books, and tried to call our families. We'd stay up as long as we could but we found ourselves, like the villagers, going to bed with the setting sun. The next morning we'd wake up and do it all over again.

When we first started working in Chisala we would go home for lunch, driving fifteen minutes to our dilapidated house on the edge of the Kawalazi Tea Plantation, which in another era had been staff housing. Sometimes we'd arrive ravenous and exhausted only to find the electricity had been cut that afternoon. With no way to cook and no time to build a fire, lunch was often PB&J and a banana before heading back to the site. This was arduous work, sometimes moving up to eight thousand bricks before noon in ninety-degree weather. A light snack wasn't enough to fill our depleted bodies and fortify us for the work ahead.

When we came dragging back to the site one afternoon, some of the committee members told us a similar story. Their houses were remote and unreachable by car, yet they were all walking home for lunch, up small, steep paths in the deep woods, quickly scarfing something down, then turning around and walking back. They were exhausted too. A lunchtime shuttle bus was not the answer. But then the solution appeared. It was so obvious! We'd hire a cook and have lunch together at the construction site. The next day, Mrs. Lungu arrived.

The first day of our shared lunch, Elias cleared out a room in a nearby cement house and brought in prepared plates for us. It was a very hospitable gesture, but without electricity the rooms were dark, and the small cutout windows meant a serious lack of cross-ventilation at the hottest point of the day. We wanted to be outside, but ever fearful for our fair skin, comparably weak constitution, and propensity for dehydration, the committee thought it wise for us to be indoors, out of the sun. As bad as it was in the sweat lodge, it was worse missing out on the ebullient scene outside under the mango tree, where George, Elias, Chisiwawa, Matthews, and Mrs. Lungu laughed and told wild stories over lunch.

After a few days of this, we asked if we could join them outside on the mat in the shade of the mango tree, lush with leaves and heavy with fruit. They looked perplexed. Wouldn't we prefer to be indoors, sheltered from the elements? Furthermore, eating indoors was reserved for esteemed people, guests of honor. We thanked them profusely for their kindness and concern but insisted we would rather be outside. It took a week or so, and a few more awkward negotiations, but one afternoon we found our plates on the mat, too. And that's where they stayed for many months to come.

People often asked us what we were finding to be the biggest challenge of living in Malawi. Was it hard for me, a woman, to be in a position of leadership? Was it hard to not have Internet at our house? Was it hard to get up and do the same grueling work day after day? Sure. But the answer that came first was always at the forefront of our minds: the hardest thing was the lack of variation in food. As people who loved to cook and eat adventurously, we found Malawian cuisine palate-numbingly boring. We ate one of the following every day: scrambled eggs, stewed beans, grilled or stewed usipa (small, anchovy-like fish). These main dishes were sometimes served with a small side of stewed leafy greens. *Every* dish was cooked and flavored with the only other readily available ingredients: tomatoes and onions. The food was bland, though blessedly, it was liberally salted. The portion size of the main and greens, what you might call "the good stuff" was no bigger than a quarter cup, served alongside a heaping three- or four-cup portion of nsima, the local starch staple made from ground maize or cassava.

After eating lunch we would lie on those bamboo mats and tell stories. George, Elias, Matthews, and Chisawawa would tell us everything we might read in the local rag—an

ugly, ongoing land dispute, the surprise marriage of a spin-
ster, the funeral for a mother who died in childbirth. They'd
tell us about the fields and gardens where they toiled three
or four hours *before* coming to work with us each morning.
They opined on Malawian politics and told us how their kids
were doing.

When it was our turn we spoke of our homes, showed
pictures of our families, and explained jokes and phrases.
Some things, though, they could not comprehend. When we
tried to explain the concept of a mortgage, they said, simply,
"Why doesn't your village headman just give you some land?
How can land be owned? It belongs to the earth." (I let Andy
take that one.) Then there was the day we happened to mention a friend who was getting unemployment benefits. When
we told them that in England and America, if you couldn't
find a job the government would give you money until you
did, they went slack-jawed. There was a long pause. Then
George spoke up: "A man is *paid* to not work?" They all
looked at one another and erupted into laughter so deep
they keeled over onto their sides. We tried to explain that
you had to pay into unemployment when you *were* gainfully
employed, but the laughter went on. With a government
that could hardly keep filling stations stocked with fuel, this
kind of largesse was plainly inconceivable. Sometimes we'd
tell stories like this and go for an hour. Other days we'd fall
effortlessly to sleep, woken by the free-roaming dogs or
chickens pecking around the mat looking for leftovers.

We started sharing this meal together for practical
reasons—it simply made more sense to stay on site and have

lunch cooked for us. But after a few weeks of eating with the committee, something shifted, something changed. Somewhere between the hand washing at the start and the nap taking near the end, we became trusted friends. The morale of the group surged, and we had the will and the capacity to persevere in the face of adversity and exhaustion as we slogged through those seemingly endless days.

A few weeks after we began taking lunch together, Elias invited us to come to his home for dinner. This was the first such invitation we'd had. This was big. Personal. We put on our best clothes, in my case a tatty skirt made from Indian saris and my least dirty T-shirt, while Andy donned a short-sleeved button-down and a pair of Bermuda shorts. We hopped in the only vehicle we had, a three-ton hauling truck, and bounced down the dirt track road through the village, hazy with the smoke of cooking fires, not knowing what to expect.

We had passed Elias's home hundreds of times on our way to town, but when we pulled up that evening we were gobsmacked. Honoring our preference for eating outside, Elias and his family had moved all the furniture from the living room and eating area of their humble grass and mud house into their front yard: old, beat-up sofas made in a nearby town, tables crafted from local lumber, large crocheted doilies covering the tables and hanging over the backs of chairs. And there sat Elias, like a king in his comically overstuffed throne, grinning like a boy on his birthday. Far from the shabby shirt and short combo he wore at the building site, Elias was positively luminous in a button-down shirt so white and starched it looked as if it had just come from the cleaners. He wore a colorful tie with black, pleated dress pants and a pair of shiny patent leather shoes.

As the Brits would say, Elias was chuffed with himself for this clever arrangement, for remembering that his guests liked to dine alfresco. As he hopped up and ran to greet the truck, my heart, which had already grown to love Elias like a quirky, hilarious uncle, felt as if it were physically swelling in my chest. Elias ushered us to our seats of honor at his outdoor table. "Ah, Maggy and Andy, you are very welcome here!"

Elias introduced us to each and every member of his extensive family, then walked us through their family crops to the small plot of twenty tobacco plants he'd been telling us about for months, the crop he believed would make him rich. In a rural, agrarian village like Chisala, jobs were few. Growing tobacco was one way to make extra money to pay for things like school fees, transportation, and home improvements. He was so proud of his twenty plants; this was the Malawian equivalent of showing us a restored antique car in a garage. As we walked back through the fields, the sun set over the great mountain in the distance that dominated the horizon from anywhere in the village.

By the time we had returned home, the table had been set, glowing with candles and lanterns. Other guests had arrived, more members of the committee as well as a few nosy neighbors curious about Elias Mkandawire's new lawn furniture. More chairs were added to the growing outdoor party, but Elias ensured that we had places of honor on the large sofa and armchair. Elias and his wife came around with a bowl and a pitcher of water to wash our hands before the food was served.

Elias's wife, eager to do her family proud and impress her foreign guests, had put much care into the preparation. She and the girls of the house—daughters, nieces, and friends, draped in their best and brightest chitenjes—carried the enamel plates and bowls in procession from fireside to tableside. Once the lids were removed, we immediately recognized each dish. It was the same fare that Mrs. Lungu had been serving us for lunch—scrambled eggs, stewed beans, and a big bowl of the rape greens we'd become quite fond of. But there was one addition to the menu. Elias had killed a chicken, something only done on special occasions: chicken for important guests, goats for weddings and funerals when a crowd needed to be fed.

Far from the bloated, translucent chicken breasts in Styrofoam and plastic at home, the village chickens were wiry and lean from running around all day, leaving their meat tough and sinewy. What they lacked in texture, though, was redeemed in taste. The meat was dark and rich, which, when stewed with tomato and onion, made for a liquid gold sauce.

It was the most memorable meal of my life. Not because the food was Zagat-rated and the place was posh, but because we had been welcomed into a circle of hospitality and love by people who did not see us as alien as at first we felt, whose only hope that night was to bring us happiness and deep pleasure. As the night closed in and the mountain disappeared in the darkness, we sat in the lamplight and I felt a pang of homesickness. Then I realized: Only an experience of true family could make me long for my family. This is what Elias and these people had become for us.

Thereafter, Elias was a little more protective of me. If we were moving bricks and someone spotted a snake in the pile, he'd order me off duty. If we were in town for supplies and I was getting a look he didn't like, he'd come quickly and stand by my side. The relationship between Elias and Andy changed, too. Though Elias was twenty years his senior, they started acting like goofy brothers.

Instinctively, we wanted to return hospitality with a welcome of our own. So Andy and I invited all our committee members and their wives and children to our house on the tea plantation for dinner.

We spent days brainstorming what to make, wanting it to be representative of our culture but also something familiar enough that they'd enjoy. Someone told us about a man in a nearby village who slaughtered pigs and sold large hunks of meat. Once we knew we could get pork, we settled on making the Malawian equivalent of an English roast dinner. Fire-roasted pork, mashed potatoes, sautéed tomatoes, green beans, and gravy made from the pork drippings, flour, and a bit of Marmite we'd brought with us from England. Local ingredients, different use.

The night arrived and Andy went down to the trading post to pick up our twenty-some guests in the flatbed of our three-ton truck. Though it was completely dilapidated and hardly furnished, most of our guests had never been in a home like ours. It was a neglected one-story colonial—bare lightbulbs hanging from the ceiling, walls peeling, cracked linoleum floors, a functioning sink, two hot plates, and an out-of-commission oven. We had flushing toilets, glass windows, ceramic plates, and utensils. Things were a bit stiff when our guests arrived, and without booze to lubricate our teetotaling guests, Andy booted up our computer to play some music.

Before leaving England, Andy had made our laptop wallpaper a glowing cityscape of London at night. It was one of those enhanced, almost fake-looking stock images, with Big Ben and the London Eye and lights reflecting on the Thames, amid a shower of shimmering city lights. Our Malawian friends had never seen anything like this before. Elias pulled his head close to the computer. "What is this?" Andy replied, "This is London. This is where I'm from." Elias struggled to find words for something so far outside the realm of anything he'd ever known. "Andy, your village," he paused, shaking his head in disbelief, ". . . it is very beautiful."

We had come here to create a maternity clinic, and that building was slowly rising from its foundation, but the gods who hover over every scrap of bread offered in love were creating something greater. The construction project was no longer the goal of our lives, it was merely the expression of our new community. What mattered now was friendship and trust. As much as I love my family—father, mother, sister—as much as I love my husband, I was beginning to understand that our little nuclear circles can never really satisfy our deepest yearnings for love and belonging. We were made for fellowship in the big human family.

Maybe it's because I was raised to put my faith in food—

around the table in my mother's kitchen, around the altar in my father's church where bread and wine were offered to all—but I know of no other way to break down barriers and bring people into communion than by inviting them to sit down at a table, on a bamboo mat in the shade of a mango tree, in an overstuffed sofa under the stars. It was our meals—*that* is what united us, fused our souls.

The menu Andy and I thought would be brilliant—an English roast dinner translated into Malawian—could have been disastrous. Half our guests that night were Christians of Muslim descent and did not eat pork. But somehow it didn't matter. In a few moments, everyone was devouring the enormous bars of Cadbury's chocolate we'd put out for dessert, always a common denominator.

With the meal over, the music cranked up and people started dancing in our barren living room. A group of women helped start the dishes. We showed them the sponges and soap we'd bought from a store in Mzuzu. Mrs. Zimwani, our mother figure and the alpha female, belly laughed and headed straight for the door with a bowl. She came back with a heaping load of sandy dirt that she flung into every dirty, caked-on pot, pan, and plate. Dirt to clean: That's either hopelessly contradictory or strangely homeopathic. Mrs. Zimwani quickly showed us which. She started scrubbing not with a sponge but *with her hand*, then held up a pot for inspection. I smiled. That sandy grit did a much better job at cleaning than our pansy-ass sponges. The music was pumping, and the party was taking on a life of its own. I stood over the sink, bumping hips with Mrs. Zimwani to the rhythm of the music, doing dishes together with dirt.

Blue Cheese-Crusted Beef Stout Pie

SERVES 8

When I came home from Malawi in the dead of winter, I craved hot home-cooked classics with rich, deep flavor. Beef stew has always been one of my favorite cold weather dishes, but with the addition of the flaky blue cheese piecrust, Mom created my *ultimate* comfort food. Lamb lovers (like me) can substitute an equal amount of cubed lamb shoulder for the beef chuck.

These days it appears that most grocery stores carry *either* 1-pound packages of frozen pearl onions *or* 9-ounce packages of creamed pearl onions. Either works. Since I can only get creamed pearl onions, my recipe calls for that. If using regular frozen pearl onions, use a 1-pound package and add an extra tablespoon of oil when sautéing the garlic and herbs and increase flour to ¼ cup.

Blue Cheese Pastry (page 303)

4 tablespoons olive oil

1 pound sliced baby bella mushrooms

3 ½ pounds beef chuck or lamb shoulder,
cut into 1 ½-inch cubes

Salt and ground black pepper

3 large garlic cloves, minced

1 teaspoon dried thyme leaves

continued on next page

2 tablespoons flour

2 tablespoons tomato paste

2 cups chicken broth

1 1/2 cups stout

2 packages (9 ounces each) frozen creamed
pearl onions

1 pound *each:* boiling potatoes and peeled carrots,
cut into bite-size chunks

2 tablespoons Worcestershire sauce

Make Blue Cheese Pastry and refrigerate. Adjust oven rack to lower-middle position and heat oven to 450°F. Heat 2 tablespoons of oil in a 5- to 6-quart Dutch oven or heavy soup kettle over medium-high heat. Add mushrooms; sauté until most of the moisture has evaporated and mushrooms start to turn brown, 5 to 6 minutes. Transfer to a bowl; set aside.

Meanwhile, drizzle beef cubes with another tablespoon of olive oil and season with salt and pepper; toss to coat. Working in two batches to avoid overcrowding, add beef chunks to hot pot and sear, turning only once, until two sides form an impressive dark brown crust, 5 to 6 minutes per batch. Transfer to a bowl; set aside.

Heat remaining tablespoon of oil in pot. Add garlic, thyme, and flour; cook until garlic is golden, almost immediately. Vigorously whisk in tomato paste, broth, and stout, and then creamed (or regular, see above) pearl onions. Bring to a simmer; continue to simmer until creamed pearl onions have just thawed. Return beef cubes to the pot. Using two potholders to protect hands, place a sheet of heavy-duty foil over pot, pressing the foil down so that it touches the stew. Seal foil completely around edges. Place lid snugly on pot and cook until juices bubble. Set pot in the oven and cook until meat is tender, 1½ hours.

While stew cooks, bring 1 inch of water to boil in a deep skillet or pot over high heat. Place potatoes and carrots in a steamer basket, season with salt, and set in pan. Cover and steam until just tender, 6 to 8 minutes.

Remove stew from oven and carefully remove foil. Stir in steamed vegetables and Worcestershire sauce. (Stew can be cooled and refrigerated up to 2 days; if refrigerated, return to a simmer before topping with pastry.)

About 45 minutes before serving, leave oven rack at lower-middle position and heat oven to 400°F. Roll Blue Cheese Pastry to 10- to 11-inch circle (check pan diameter). Place pastry over stew; set pot in oven and bake, uncovered, until stew is bubbly and pastry is golden brown, about 30 minutes. (For a richer colored pastry, turn on broiler and continue to cook 1 to 2 minutes longer.) Spoon into soup plates and serve.

Blue Cheese Pastry

ENOUGH FOR A SINGLE-CRUST 9-INCH PIE

1 ¼ cups all-purpose flour

½ teaspoon salt

1 ½ teaspoons sugar

continued on next page

1 stick (8 tablespoons) frozen unsalted butter,
quartered lengthwise and cut into
1/2-inch pieces

3 ounces crumbled blue cheese

1/3 cup ice water

Pulse flour, salt, and sugar in a food processor to blend. Add butter; process with 12 to 14 one-second pulses until mixture resembles coarse meal with pea-size butter pieces. Add blue cheese; process with 2 to 3 more one-second pulses until incorporated. Transfer mixture to a medium bowl; sprinkle ice water over mixture and combine using a fork until mixture starts to come together. Switching to hands, form mixture into a ball, pressing dough onto the side of the bowl and sprinkling in a little more water, if necessary, to get dough to form a solid ball. Wrap dough in plastic and press into a 4-inch disc. Refrigerate at least 30 minutes or up to 2 days.

A SECOND HELPING

UNTIL YOU LOSE SOMEONE YOU LOVE, YOU DON'T REALIZE what a milestone that first year will be. The first time you want to tell him something and he isn't around to talk. The first time you call and the message on the machine isn't his voice anymore. The first time you visit not a home but a cemetery on his birthday. The first Thanksgiving and Christmas meals made without him in the kitchen, shared without him at the table.

This year marked Granny's eighty-ninth birthday and her first complete year without Papa. It has been a tough year for all of us, but especially for her. We lost a beloved father and grandfather, but losing a life partner is another kind of grief entirely. None of us could bear the thought of Granny at her retirement facility celebrating nearly nine decades over a plate of institutional food and a slice of store-bought cake. So we all made the pilgrimage south—Pam from Connecticut, Maggy from New York City, Sharon from Atlanta.

Granny's appetite and taste buds are tempted by precious little these days. Pam, knowing what her mother loves best, planned a birthday menu featuring old favorites. The centerpiece of the meal was thick steaks smothered in sautéed mushrooms and a rich, dark pan sauce. Nestled alongside the meat were roasted asparagus, crispy garlic bread, and, of course, big Idaho potatoes and Vidalia onions sliced, arranged in foil, and baked until caramelized and fall-apart tender.

Granny, who weighs about ninety pounds if she's carrying an oversized suitcase, usually picks at her food and tries to palm it off on other people. Not tonight. At her birthday fete she was the only one to clean her plate, and even then she proceeded to pick fat, juicy mushrooms off other people's abandoned dishes. When it came time for dessert, we all assumed she'd blow out the candles and cry uncle, but Granny surprised everyone by tucking into a hefty slice of Sharon's carrot cake.

Quietly, we were all expecting it to be something of a somber evening, but it turned out to be the most fun we'd had together in months. Maggy and Sharon made sure that Granny had balloons, a banner, and a big gaudy pin declaring her the "Birthday Girl." Gwen and Patricia, Granny's nieces, who can always be counted on for a good time, brought their best jokes and family stories. We started out giggling that we'd probably set off the fire alarms in this retirement community trying to get a good sear on our steaks, and we didn't stop laughing all night. As Granny ended the evening pilfering food off our plates, we were absolutely roaring over her unprecedented food consumption. Where was she putting it all?! Unlike the days after the funeral, when our laughter was desperate, bittersweet, and

holding back tears, tonight it was untinged with sorrow—
simple and sweet.

Granny loved the meal and the quiet pleasure of watching her daughter and granddaughters prepare it. She
thought the best had already been served, but we had secretly saved the chef d'oeuvre. As the meal was winding
down, Maggy asked if Granny was ready for dessert. Granny
nodded. Maggy reached into her purse and sheepishly extracted a blurry ultrasound photo, placing it on the plate in
front of her grandmother. Granny cocked her head in momentary disbelief. "This," Maggy announced in the most
deadpan voice she could muster, "is a portrait of your great-
grandson." Granny looked at Pam, then back at the photo,
and let fly her signature squeal, delirious with delight. For
this woman battling the specter of cancer, that grainy black-
and-white image represented not only a baby, but a promise.
That little kidney bean with long legs and a strong heartbeat
promised a next generation—children who will be spoon-
fed good food and great love until they are old enough to
help create that food and share that love with others.

Granny now has a new purpose: Live to see that baby boy.
But even if her life ends before his begins, she knows that
our hands spooning squash and peas into his toothless grin
bear a love much older and deeper than our own. It's her
love and Papa's love. It's Mama Skipper's and Juliaette's. It's
the love we have shared together through meal after meal,
generation after generation. A love that finds its life in the
kitchen.

Granny got a little quiet when she heard that the baby
will bear her husband's middle name: Collins. We all got a

little quiet, too, actually. The whole evening—full of big laughs, great big appetites, big steaks, and big slices of cake—felt positively saturated with the oversized spirit of Flynn Collins Skipper. He must have been there, we all said, smiling and belly-laughing right along with us, urging us to add a little more butter to the pan. If, along with that shared name, this new son carries with him anything of that big-loving man, we will all be blessed, and the tradition will live on at least one more generation.

ACKNOWLEDGMENTS

WE THREE COOKS ARE GRATEFUL TO THOSE WHO HAVE HELPED US IN life, online, and in print:

Our editor, Pamela Cannon, who considered our original cookbook proposal and then empowered us to write our stories;

David Anderson, who took our work up one big notch;

Our agent and mother of four daughters, Stacey Glick, who believed this mother-daughter team had something to say;

Erika Pineda-Ghanny, our first blogging friend and Fourth Many Cook;

Ree Drummond, a.k.a Pioneer Woman, who helped us get up and running online and who has encouraged and promoted our work over the years;

The Big Potluck crew: Rod and Deb Smith, Chris and Karen Thornton, Sabrina Modelle, Brian Samuels, Kathi Johnson, and Brooke Burton—who have seen us at our best and worst and who live out the ideals of the "food community."

Our photographer, William Taufic, who took not just one photo but scores that three women actually liked.

pam

MY COUSINS, PATRICIA GEROSOLINA AND GWEN SADLER, AND MY aunt Dot—the Golden Girls—who care for my mother when I'm not there.

To my friends at AARP who encourage me bi-weekly to write about what I love.

To my editors at *Runner's World* who give me quarterly space in their pages and feature me regularly.

maggy

MURIEL MAYHEW ("NANNY"), WHO LET ME LEARN BY HER SIDE AS SHE made the great British classics like Victoria sponge and traditional Sunday roasts, so that even after we left England I could still make her grandson's favorites.

sharon

MY HUSBAND, ANTHONY, WHO CHALLENGES, TEACHES, AND PARTners with me in the kitchen every single day. I am thankful for his discerning palate, unflagging energy, and honest critique as we developed and tested every recipe that I have included in this book.

I am also indebted to the women of *Fine Cooking* magazine—especially Susie Middleton, Denise Mickelsen, Sarah Breckenridge, Juli Roberts, and Laurie Buckle—who took a chance on a naïve young woman looking for a job and made time to help her grow. Thank you for never making me feel silly or provincial, even though I was surely both. Thank you for teaching me, for encouraging me to lift my voice, and for sharing your lives and your food with me for two short, but life-changing, years. I will always proudly count *FC* as a vital part of my culinary education.

New York Times bestselling author of seven books, PAM ANDERSON is AARP's official food expert and a *Runner's World* contributing columnist. She is the former executive editor at *Cook's Illustrated* and food columnist at *USA Weekend*. Along with her daughters, Maggy and Sharon, she blogs at threemanycooks.com. She lives in Darien, Connecticut, and Springtown, Pennsylvania, with her husband, David.

MAGGY KEET graduated from University of Exeter in 2005 with a degree in English literature and sociology. After several years in the social work field, she went back to school, graduating in 2009 with a master's degree in globalization and international development from the University of London's School of Oriental and African Studies. After living in Malawi and building a maternity clinic, she moved with her husband, Andy, to New York City, where she now works fundraising for Haiti with the Development Office of the Episcopal Church.

SHARON DAMELIO, the younger of Pam's two daughters, graduated from Williams College in 2007 with a degree in English and Classics, and spent the next two years working at *Fine Cooking* magazine as the assistant web editor. She graduated from Yale Divinity School with a master of divinity in 2012 and now lives with her husband, Anthony, in Atlanta, Georgia, where she works at a nonprofit that provides emergency services and job readiness training to homeless and near-homeless individuals.

A B O U T   T H E   T Y P E

This book was set in Granjon, a modern recutting of a typeface produced under the direction of George W. Jones (1860–1942), who based
Granjon's design upon the letterforms of Claude Garamond (1480–
1561). The name was given to the typeface as a tribute to the typo-
graphic designer Robert Granjon (1513–89).